*Stephen D. Brookfield*

# The Skillful
# Teacher

# The Skillful Teacher

*On Technique, Trust, and Responsiveness in the Classroom*

Jossey-Bass Publishers

San Francisco • Oxford • 1990

THE SKILLFUL TEACHER
*On Technique, Trust, and Responsiveness in the Classroom*
  by Stephen D. Brookfield

Copyright © 1990 by:    Jossey-Bass Inc., Publishers
                        350 Sansome Street
                        San Francisco, California 94104
                                &
                        Jossey-Bass Limited
                        Headington Hill Hall
                        Oxford OX3 0BW

**Library of Congress Cataloging-in-Publication Data**

Brookfield, Stephen D.
    The skillful teacher: on technique, trust, and responsiveness in
the classroom/Stephen D. Brookfield.—1st ed.
        p.     cm.—(The Jossey-Bass higher education series)
    Includes bibliographical references (p.    ) and index.
    ISBN 1-55542-267-5
    1. College teaching.   2. Brookfield, Stephen.   3. College
teachers—United States.     I. Title   II. Series.
LB2331.B68      1990
378.1'25—dc20                                              90-40387
                                                              CIP


Manufactured in the United States of America

The paper in this book meets the guidelines for
permanence and durability of the Committee on
Production Guidelines for Book Longevity of the
Council on Library Resources.


JACKET DESIGN BY WILLI BAUM




FIRST EDITION

*Code 9087*

*The Jossey-Bass*
*Higher Education Series*

Consulting Editor
Adult and Continuing Education

Alan B. Knox
*University of Wisconsin, Madison*

*This book is lovingly dedicated to
the memory of my father, David Brookfield.
In the values he taught me, and the ways
in which he taught them, lie the
inspiration for much of my work.*

# Contents

# Preface

In 1990, I celebrated my twentieth anniversary as a college teacher by completing this book. My intention in writing it was to tell the real story of teaching. This story, which is full of unexpected twists and turns, unpredicted events, and unlooked-for surprises, is one of complexities, uncertainties, and passions. I wanted to tell the story in a way that communicated these passions, so that teachers could recognize their own emotional selves in its pages. I wanted to convey the marvelous messiness of classroom life and to explore the ways in which teaching is a deeply emotional process; to provide guidelines on how to thrive on the chaos of teaching, how to celebrate its diversity, and how to strive for the psychological, political, and pedagogical balances that all college teachers seek; to show college teachers as flesh-and-blood human beings, full of enthusiasms and frailties.

*The Skillful Teacher* is really a survival manual. It is meant to help college teachers work their way through the recurring problems and dilemmas they inevitably face in their practice. It is designed to reduce the feelings of inadequacy and guilt that all college teachers at some time or another experience because they think (mistakenly) that they are the only ones who find that things are beyond their control in the classroom, while all their colleagues appear to be calm paragons of pedagogical virtue. The book is partly a response to all those days when I felt frustrated because events in my classroom refused to follow the scripts I had written for them. These were the days when students did not leave my classes wreathed in smiles of self-actualized gratitude, but rather with expressions of anger, confusion, or resentment.

When I went through such days of confusion and debilitation, I needed a book that would focus on dilemmas, uncertainties, and intractable problems as much as on success stories—focus on how you survive and flourish when things seem to be going wrong, rather than on how things are always supposed to go right. (When things were going right, I didn't need such a book—I was too busy enjoying myself.) On difficult days, I wanted a book that would not lie to me, that would tell me the truth about how tough teaching sometimes is, and that would give me ways of analyzing my problems and finding solutions to them. In reading this book, I would feel better about myself and my teaching and would be able to summon up the courage and energy to go back into class the next day with a sense of renewal and purpose.

In writing *The Skillful Teacher*, then, I set some major problems for myself as an author. I had to ground whatever I wrote in an easily recognized, commonly shared experience of teaching. I had to write in a way that would encourage, strengthen, and inspire. Also, I had to display enough understanding of the diverse contexts of college teaching, and the problems typically experienced by college teachers, to be able to offer insights, advice, and practical suggestions that would go beyond reassuring clichés or banal generalities. In effect, these three leitmotifs—the experiential, the inspirational, and the practical—run through the entire book. They dominate its organization, comprise its major themes, and represent its chief purposes.

I have three major aims for the book on the experiential plane. The first is to present a picture of teaching that seems truthful to readers. I drew this picture not primarily from my own biography, but from accounts of the teaching experience collected from teachers by numerous researchers, myself included. These accounts focused on the unpredictability of college teaching, on its frustrations as well as its joys, and on the sense of ambiguity that sometimes seems to be the only given on which teachers can depend. The experience of being a teacher is the explicit focus of Chapter One, but the major elements of this experience are discussed throughout the book. The second experiential aim was to place students' experience of learning at the forefront of teachers' minds. This is the central concern of Chapters Three, Four, and Five, all of which explore how teachers can understand their students' experience of learning and how they can make their teaching more responsive to it. Finally, I wanted to make sure that I addressed the noninstructional dilemmas teachers consistently raised in my workshops, courses, and faculty development programs. The chapters on understanding and overcoming resistance to learning, on building trust with learners, and on taking into account the political realities of teaching all spring from this concern.

On the inspirational plane, I wanted to rekindle the sense of the importance and purpose of college teaching—the belief that college teachers can and do make a difference to their students and to society outside the classroom—which has been assailed from all sides in the last two decades. The 1970s were the heyday of radical pessimism, of the belief of reproduction theorists such as Bourdieu and Passerson (1977) and Bowles and Gintis (1976) that educational institutions were little more than factories for the production and distribution of knowledge and that they mirrored the fundamental inequities of capitalist society as a whole. The stratified, segmented nature of organized education, said these theorists, meant that schools and colleges were only machine shops for equipping and socializing students for their structurally determined niches in the labor market. This view effectively reduced teachers to being either helpless or conniving assembly line supervisors. In the 1980s, higher education faced a different attack from those critics who, like Bloom (1987) and Hirsch (1987), saw college teachers as hopelessly lost in Dewey-inspired relativism.

In *The Skillful Teacher*, I add my voice to those resisting both these interpretations. I reject the pessimism inherent in the reproductionist view that education is wholly determined by, and responsive to, the demands of capitalism. Resistance theorists such as Apple (1982) and Giroux (1983, 1988) have argued convincingly that classrooms are battle sites in which the claims of different value systems are contested and in which a plurality of perspectives are possible. In works such as those by Greene (1986), Daloz (1986), Gamson and Associates (1984), and Shor (1987), we find hopeful descriptions of how college classrooms can be arenas of critical thinking in which students' sense of agency is nurtured.

I reject also the conservative, apocalyptic analyses of higher education that hark back to an era of classically derived verities. These analyses fail to match the complex, multicultural ambiguity of contemporary adulthood. They serve only to support the wishful thinking of those who want to believe that college teaching boils down to the enthusiastic inculcation in students of universally agreed-on objective facts and the appreciation of higher truths. This is a cocktail party view of higher education (Brookfield, 1987b), in response to which students dedicate themselves to becoming more and more adept at name dropping, at alluding to facts, names, places, dates, and concepts that demonstrate their cultural literacy or intellectual sophistication.

Finally, on the practical level, I wanted to write a book that would take the major demands, dilemmas, and problems of college teaching and analyze them in an informative and helpful way. It would be easy to write a book long on experience and inspiration but short on practicalities. To avoid doing that, I analyzed the questions, issues, and concerns about the practice of college teaching that have been raised over the years by teachers who have participated in my professional development workshops. These questions, issues, and concerns provided the organizing focus for the chapters on lecturing, discussion, simulation and role play, evaluation, overcoming resistance to learning, building trust, and skillful teaching. I tried to fill the chapters with advice and suggestions on all aspects of those activities, and to give recognizable examples of typical problems and potential solutions.

Unlike other standard texts in the area of college teaching, this is a book written from an adult learning and adult education perspective. I have often been puzzled by the distinction that some academics draw between higher education and adult education. To me, college teaching is the teaching of people who are partially or fully immersed in the experience of adulthood. In this sense, college education is adult education. Yet the rich literature on adult learning and adult education is rarely acknowledged, let alone drawn upon, in most works on college teaching. In my years of teaching students in a variety of college settings, I have, to my mind, been practicing a form of adult education. So the distinctive perspective of *The Skillful Teacher,* and what I think is its unique contribution, is the recognition of college students as the adults they really are and the bringing to bear on college teaching of insights drawn from the research, theory, and philosophy of adult learning and adult education.

Wanting to write in a sympathetic way about the travails, pleasures, and serendipities of college teaching, I have adopted a particular tone in my prose, which stands in marked contrast to the style of my other books. I have deliberately excluded, as much as was humanly possible for me, scholarly references to the research literature on teaching and learning. I wanted to communicate as directly and personally as I could to practicing teachers, and I felt that writing in the traditional scholarly vein—with every assertion and suggestion supported by copious references to the research literature—would slow the pace and decrease the book's accessibility without offering much advantage. The book that I used to want to read for sustenance, advice, and encouragement when I had come home from a bad day in the classroom would not be peppered with scholarly references.

In *The Skillful Teacher,* I have tried to write as I would speak, using the familiar *you* and the personal *I* throughout the text, since it seemed to me that these forms would cut through the distance between reader and author that is created by more traditional academic prose styles. It is my hope that this conversational and personal tone will connect most directly with those trying to grapple with the challenges and crises of college teaching.

## Audience

The audience I had in mind while writing this book was all college educators for whom teaching students is a major part of their professional responsibility. Although I draw examples throughout the book from my experience teaching at the college level, much of this material will be of interest to upper-level high school teachers. That abstract concept so beloved of preface writers—the typical reader—did not really exist for me, because the book can be read by a variety of people, for diverse purposes. I hope it will be helpful to beginning college teachers who are wondering how they are going to get through the next day, much less the rest of the semester. I hope that teachers who are experts in their subject matter but who have not really thought about issues of teaching and learning will find that it focuses their minds on things they need to attend to and suggests how they can start to do this. I hope that relatively experienced teachers who are caught in dilemmas they seem to encounter over and over again in their professional lives will find here insights and suggestions on how to alter their situations. I hope that those who have been teaching for a long time and are suffering from a sense of torpor and routine will find something to renew them and to remind them why they became college teachers in the first place. Finally, I hope that teachers everywhere who are dogged by the suspicion that they fall woefully short of being the calm, controlled, skilled orchestrators of learning spoken about on faculty development days (and in the pages of textbooks like this one) will feel reassured by the common experience of teaching I have depicted.

## Overview of the Contents

The book begins with a chapter on the experience of teaching. Drawing on studies of teachers' thinking, Chapter One emphasizes the chaotic unpredictability of teaching and the ways in which this activity is viscerally experienced. I discuss the risks endemic to the profession and suggest ways in which teachers can survive—and flourish—in the unpredictable ambiguities of the classroom. The chapter ends with a discussion of how teachers grow into their own truths about college teaching.

Chapter Two focuses on the need to clarify the purpose of teaching. I argue that all teachers must develop a critical rationale to guide their practice—a sense of where they are going and why it's important to go there. Doing this is personally, politically, professionally, and pedagogically important. I propose as the most appropriate rationale for college teaching the development of critical thinking. I also introduce the concept of critically responsive teaching—teaching that is guided by a critical rationale but that adapts to students' experience of learning and to the contextual variables of classroom life.

The theme of critically responsive teaching is further developed in Chapters Three, Four, and Five. In these three chapters, I discuss how teachers can discover ways in which students experience learning, I present what research reveals to be some of the typical rhythms of learning, and I analyze how teachers can respond to, and build on, these rhythms.

Chapter Three describes how to use critical incidents and learning journals to understand how students experience learning and how they perceive teachers' behaviors. I advocate teachers' studying their own biographies as learners as an important way of gaining insights into their own teaching, and I outline how experiencing learning can become a valuable approach to faculty development.

Chapter Four presents insights from critical incident responses, learning journals, and research reports documenting how students experience learning.

Chapter Five discusses how teachers can best adjust their practice to take these rhythms of learning into account.

In Chapter Six I consider the lecture—the method of college teaching that is probably the most frequently used and abused. I set forth the purposes for which lectures are most appropriate and then present suggestions on how lectures can be made as enlivening and critically stimulating as possible.

Chapters Seven and Eight examine how teachers can make sure that the discussions they lead are fair, focused, and respectfully conducted. In these chapters I present some important preparatory steps that discussion leaders should take and consider some of the most common difficulties they face. I offer guidelines on getting discussions started, dealing with the overly talkative, encouraging silent members, reducing analytical confusion, avoiding definitive summaries, and protecting minority viewpoints.

In Chapter Nine, I look at when and how simulations and role play should be used. I give examples of both these teaching approaches and of some of their most interesting variants, such as critical debate and role reversal.

How to give helpful evaluations—ones from which students can learn—is the focus of Chapter Ten. The chapter opens with examples of helpful and unhelpful evaluations, identifies the chief characteristics of helpful evaluations, and suggests how teachers can improve their skills at giving evaluations to students.

Chapter Eleven deals with those most complex of all teaching questions—Why do some students so strongly resist learning? and What should teachers' responses to this resistance be? I review the most common reasons students resist learning and present very specific actions teachers can take in response.

The importance of trust as the foundation for all significant teaching and learning is discussed in Chapter Twelve. Here I outline the crucial components of teacher credibility and teacher authenticity and review the important steps teachers can consider for building trust with students.

In Chapter Thirteen I examine the ways in which political factors—both inside and outside colleges—affect the practice of teaching. I offer some strategies for political survival and conclude by analyzing the political values and purposes of college teaching.

Chapter Fourteen summarizes, in the form of seventeen truths about skillful teaching, most of the main themes that have emerged in the previous thirteen chapters. The chapter opens with a discussion of how people define effectiveness and ends with a caution against uncritically accepting my seventeen truths.

## Acknowledgments

My most important acknowledgment is of the teachers, students, workshop participants, conference attendees, and colleagues who have, in their different ways, asked that most difficult of all questions for educators to answer: "Well, this is all very nice in theory, but what happens when it doesn't work in practice?" The problems they have posed, the issues they have raised, and the concerns they have expressed have provided the impetus for much of what I have included. On a more practical note, I must thank the administration of Teachers College, Columbia University, for providing the sabbatical leave (my one and only in twenty years of teaching) necessary for me to put these thoughts and insights down on paper. I also commiserate with my colleagues in the adult education graduate program at the college who took over my responsibilities while I was on leave. Not only did they have to endure a series of postcards from increasingly exotic locations, but they also had to put up with my unashamed grins of relief as I saw them grapple with the professorial and administrative complexities I had put aside during that time. So thanks for their forbearance go to Elizabeth Kasl, May Kenn, Theresa Lewis, Victoria Marsick, and Jack Mezirow.

During my sabbatical, I had the good fortune to be invited to spend some months as a visiting fellow at the Institute for Technical and Adult Teacher Education (I.T.A.T.E.) at the Sydney College of Advanced Education (now the Faculty of Adult Education, University of Technology, Sydney) in Sydney, Australia. By the time I left Sydney, I felt that everyone in Eastern Australia must have heard everything I had ever thought or uttered about teaching and learning. In the process, however, I was able to test and refine many of the insights in this book under the critically sympathetic gaze of the experienced faculty there. Thanks to Keith Foster, Paul Hager, Leonie Jennings, Sue Knights, Val Levy, Larry Lucas, Rod Macdonald, Roger Morris, Mike Newman, Geoff Scott, Mark Tennant, Rosie Wickert, and "friends" of I.T.A.T.E., such as David Boud, Philip Candy, Peter Poulson, and John Wellings.

As is always the case, Alan Knox and the anonymous and semi-anonymous reviewers of Jossey-Bass told me some hard truths about earlier drafts of this book. Their insights, unflinchingly given, helped make this a much tighter, more focused book. Jon Van Til was especially helpful in this regard. Finally, as ever, I am thankful for the reality testing that Kim Miller and Molly Miller Brookfield gave the manuscript. If Kim could read it without laughing (in the wrong places, that is) and Molly could listen to it without crying, then I knew there must be something worthwhile there.

# The Author

Stephen D. Brookfield is professor in the Department of Higher and Adult Education at Teachers College, Columbia University, in New York City. He received his B.A. degree (1970) from Coventry Polytechnic in modern studies, his M.A. degree (1974) from the University of Reading in sociology, and his Ph.D. degree (1980) from the University of Leicester in adult education. He also holds a postgraduate diploma (1971) from the University of London, Chelsea College, in modern social and cultural studies and a postgraduate diploma (1977) from the University of Nottingham in adult education.

Brookfield's main research activities have been in the fields of adult learning, critical thinking, and teaching. He has been national chair of the Adult Education Research Conference of North America (1985) and a member of the national executive committee of the Association for Recurrent Education in the United Kingdom (1981). He serves on the editorial and advisory boards of *Adult Education Quarterly* (United States), the *Canadian Journal for Studies in Adult Education, Studies in Continuing Education* (Australia), and *Convergence: A Journal of International Adult Education* (International Council of Adult Education).

Brookfield has held teaching appointments in colleges of further, technical, adult, and higher education and at three universities. He has been a visiting professor at the University of British Columbia in Vancouver, Canada, and a visiting fellow of the Institute for Technical and Adult Teacher Education, Sydney College of Advanced Education, Sydney, Australia.

He has run numerous faculty development workshops on teaching, learning, and critical thinking at colleges and universities in the United States, Canada, Great Britain, and Australia, and he has delivered many keynote addresses at national and regional conferences on adult and higher education.

He has twice won the Cyril O. Houle World Award for Literature in Adult Education: in 1986 for his book *Understanding and Facilitating Adult Learning: A Comprehensive Analysis of Principles and Effective Practices* (1986) and in 1989 for *Developing Critical Thinkers: Challenging Adults to Explore Alternative Ways of Thinking and Acting* (1987a). *Understanding and Facilitating Adult Learning* also won the 1986 Imogene E. Okes Award for Outstanding Research in Adult Education. All these awards were presented by the American Association for Adult and Continuing Education. His other books include *Adult Learners, Adult Education and the Community* (1984), *Self-Directed Learning: From Theory to Practice* (1985), *Learning Democracy: Eduard Lindeman on Adult Education and Social Change* (1987), and *Training Educators of Adults: The Theory and Practice of Graduate Adult Education* (1988).

# CHAPTER ONE

# Teaching:
# A Complex and
# Passionate Experience

Passion, hope, doubt, fear, exhilaration, weariness, colleague-ship, loneliness, glorious defeats, hollow victories, and, above all, the certainties of surprise and ambiguity—how can one begin to capture the reality of teaching in a single word or phrase? A book that addresses this reality and focuses on the actual experience of teaching must eschew simple descriptors or neat conceptualizations. For the truth is that teaching is frequently a gloriously messy pursuit in which surprise, shock, and risk are endemic. The idiosyncratic messiness of classroom reality is as far removed from the orderly textbook version (in which teachers carefully apply systematic methods in the pursuit of unequivocal objectives) as the inconvenient messiness of real-life marriage is from the neat television sit-com versions such as "Ozzie and Harriet" and "Family Ties."

## Experiencing Teaching

Teaching is experienced as deeply emotive and bafflingly cha-otic (Salzberger-Wittenberg, Henry, and Osborne, 1983). As is evident from surveys of the experience of teaching (Tulasie-wicz and Adams, 1989), and particularly of teachers' thought processes (Calderhead, 1987; Clark, 1988), most teachers are all too aware of this chaos. Not surprisingly, they report that they experience their practice as complex, uncertain, and riddled with dilemmas (Elbow, 1986). In the midst of teaching, teachers make a dazzlingly quick series of judgments about what to do next or how to respond to unforeseen eventualities (Calderhead, 1984). These intuitive and immediate judgments are based not on calmly reasoned discussions that occurred months before but on viscerally felt, "gut" instincts concerning which actions best fit certain situations. They are informed by recollections of similar situations experienced in the past. Even as we react to a situation we are scanning our memories for incidents that felt like the ones we face and that might provide some guidance on how to respond. This process occurs almost instantaneously so that reflection is perceived as concurrent with action. It is acting mindfully or acting thinkingly.

Teaching is the educational equivalent of white-water rafting. Periods of apparent calm are interspersed with sudden frenetic turbulence. Boredom alternates with excitement, reflection with action. As we successfully negotiate rapids fraught with danger, we feel a sense of self-confident exhilaration. As we start downstream after capsizing, our self-confidence is shaken and we are awash in self-doubt. All teachers sooner or later capsize, and all teachers worth their salt regularly ask themselves whether or not they are doing the right thing. Experiencing regular episodes of hesitation, disappointment, and ego-deflation is quite normal. Indeed, the awareness of painful dilemmas in our practice, and the readiness to admit that we are hurting from experiencing these, is an important indicator that we are critically alert. If you deny experiencing such dilemmas, you are either exhibiting denial on a massive scale or getting through each class on automatic pilot. As Jersild (1955) noted in his classic study, teaching is an experience in which one commonly feels lonely, anxious, alienated, and abused.

So classrooms are often arenas of confusion where the teachers are gladiators of ambiguity (Jackson, 1990). Just when we think we have anticipated every eventuality, something unexpected happens eliciting new responses and causing us to question our assumptions about the nature of teaching. Yet feeling unsure, realizing that our actions some-times contradict our words, or admitting that we are not in control of every event in our practice are anathema to many of us. We believe that unless we anticipate every eventuality and respond appropriately we are failing. Appearing con-fused, hesitant, or baffled seems a sign of weakness. And admitting that we feel tired, unmotivated, or bored seems a betrayal of the humanitarian zest we are supposed to exhibit.

When all these feelings arise, as they are bound to with alarming regularity, two responses are typically called forth. One is to be weighed down with guilt at our apparent failure to embody the idealized characteristics of a properly humane, omniscient, perfectly balanced teacher. The other is to deny that anything untoward has happened, to say, in effect, that our performance has been exemplary but that our students, colleagues, or superiors are too narrow-minded, or unsophis-ticated, to see this clearly. The most reasonable response, which falls somewhere between these two extremes of self-flagellating guilt and self-delusional denial, requires accept-ing that when one is traversing terrains of ambiguity, episodes of apparent chaos and contradiction are inevitable. It requires recognizing that the old army acronym SNAFU most approx-imates the activity of teaching: "Situation Normal, All Fouled Up," to put it politely.

New teachers soon learn to expect ambiguity and unpre-dictability (Fink, 1984; Eble, 1988). They quickly come to realize that the role model of the competent teacher as a peda-gogically poised individual, anticipating all possible educa-tional eventualities and responding appropriately to them, is distorted and unrealistic. For teachers trained to believe that classrooms are rational sites of intellectual analysis, the shock they experience at crossing borders of chaos into zones of ambiguity is intensely disorienting (Lowman, 1984). It is an experiential sauna bath, a plunge from the reassuring warmth of believing that classrooms are ordered arenas governed by reason into the ice-cold reality of wrestling with the alarming complexities of teaching and learning.

The immediate reaction to this immersion in reality is

often a rejection of all educational theories and concepts. These are cynically dismissed as unrealistic and irrelevant artefacts peddled by insecure, failed teachers who hide their inability to survive classroom chaos by taking refuge inside a teacher-education program. Sometimes a different reaction occurs as teachers deny the messiness of educational reality and cling stubbornly to basic theoretical tenets despite all evidence to the contrary. This book describes a more productive response than either of these reactions, for it explores the balance between developing a guiding vision that informs our teaching and responding flexibly to different contexts and unanticipated events.

## Surviving the Experience of College Teaching

At a very basic level, college teaching involves surviving the experience of chaotic ambiguity described in the previous section. Because this book deals chiefly with problems of practice, it is important to affirm at the outset how critical your own survival is. You may feel that concentrating on the need to survive is selfish and narcissistic and that it diverts emotional energy from where your focus should be—on your students. A concern for one's own survival seems to contradict the spirit of humanistic concern and learner-centered empathy prized by so many college teachers. Yet the risks incurred in college teaching are so dangerous that all teachers must strive to reduce them to a reasonable level.

Five risks are typically faced by college teachers: burning out, getting fired, becoming crucified on the cross of imagined perfectability, aspiring to a fruitless martyrdom, and falling victim to a cynical pessimism about the possibility of ever making a difference in the lives of students. If you don't regard your own survival as at least as important as the development of your students, then you will sooner or later fall victim to one of these risks. And if you do burn out, get fired, become crucified, sacrifice your position fruitlessly, or are consumed by pessimism about the limits on your influence, then you are no good to anyone, least of all to your students.

So paying attention to your survival as a teacher is not a narcissistic conceit; it is a fundamental necessity that you owe to yourself and to your students.

The benefits of paying serious attention to your own survival as a teacher are enormous. You increase your chances of experiencing the frequent lows of classroom life in a way which does not destroy your morale. You are more likely to be able to withstand students' expressions of anger and resentment when you're expecting their gratitude. You are better placed to acknowledge failure as a necessary part of the experimentation central to all good teaching. You can come home after a day of frustration and disappointment and say to yourself, "Some days you eat the bear, some days the bear eats you." You stand a better chance of achieving a balance between stoically accepting the unpredictable vicissitudes of classroom life and being inspired by an organizing vision of where you should be going. Most important of all, perhaps, you'll get a decent night's sleep. As you reflect on the insights for survival discussed in the following paragraphs, I hope that some unnecessary sources of anxiety about your performance will be removed and that your convictions about the value of your efforts will be strengthened.

***Don't Misinterpret Poor Evaluations.*** Having our practice evaluated is something we experience emotionally and something which, to varying degrees, we all fear. In particular, receiving a poor evaluation of your efforts from your students is profoundly debilitating and depressing. We can dismiss poor evaluations from our superiors or peers as being inspired by jealousy, but poor evaluations from learners are taken much more to heart. One of the most common mistakes teachers make when they receive evaluations from students is to focus all their attention on those that disparage their efforts (even when these are in the minority) and to neglect those that praise them. A curious mix of perfectionism and masochism in many teachers (myself included) leads them to grant a disproportionate credibility to the judgment of those critical of their efforts and to discredit the judgment of those who praise them. It is as if we say to ourselves, "Anyone who disparages me possesses a superior level of analytical insight, and anyone who is naive enough to praise me obviously lacks critical sophistication." This mistrust of students who acknowledge our efforts may spring from an admirable desire not to be seduced into always seeking students' approval, but it can be taken too far.

In judging the success of their efforts, teachers frequently equate students' expressions of satisfaction with pedagogic excellence. We believe that if students are pleased with us then we have done well and that if they are displeased then we have failed. This is a fundamental, and dangerous, misconception. Admittedly, students' dissatisfaction with what has transpired can indicate serious problems. But this is not necessarily the case. Before your morale plunges after receiving a poor evaluation from a student, consider the following insight: Many learners, as Chapter Four indicates, regard as the most significant and transformative learning episodes those which, as they were experienced, were painful or tinged with trauma. In the immediate aftermath of such episodes, which is when most evaluations are conducted, there is likely to be some resentment and anger directed by students at the perceived cause of their discomfort, that is, at you, the teacher.

So when you receive a poor evaluation of your efforts from a student, remember that it may signal that you have done something very valuable rather than indicating the opposite. It may mean that you have asked students to do something significant but personally discomforting. For example, you may have challenged students to scrutinize the uncritically accepted assumptions underlying their ideas and actions (always a difficult and discomforting process) rather than leaving them within the confines of their comfortable, but narrowly constraining, paradigms. This is not something students are always likely to thank you for while it is happening. You may have asked students to try to develop a new skill—such as suggesting that people examine their ideas more critically or asking domineering team members to learn how to listen carefully to the contributions of other participants—that these students do not feel they need. Even if you are convinced that learning something new and difficult is in a student's best long-term interest, you must expect that the strength of your conviction will be matched equally by the strength of a student's resentment.

The significance of your actions as a teacher are often not appreciated by students until long after the educational activity is over. At the end of a given learning episode, students may well conclude, despite your best efforts to persuade them otherwise, that the skills they have learned, the knowledge they have acquired, or the insights they have realized are essentially irrelevant to their lives. It is only months, or even years, later that they find themselves in situations in which the significance of a learning episode becomes apparent, Yet, at the time they are asked to evaluate the usefulness of this episode (and by implication, the quality of your teaching), they may have no way of judging how well these skills or insights will help them flourish in, and make sense of, subsequent situations.

*Be Wary of the Myth of the Perfect Teacher.* Teachers who care passionately about their practice can easily become obsessed with a role model of the exemplary teacher. This role model offers a perfectly balanced composite of admired behaviors and personality traits. The perfect teacher comes to be seen as a blending of something like one-third Phil Donahue or Oprah Winfrey, one-third Ted Koppel or Judy Woodruff, and one-third David Letterman or Lily Tomlin. In other words, they see the ideal teacher as a mix of humanistic empathy (Donahue and Winfrey), critical questioning (Koppel and Woodruff), and sharp, contextually appropriate humor (Letterman and Tomlin). If you subscribe to something like this vision of perfection, it is but a short step to believing that realizing this vision will make you a good teacher. You start to ask yourself, How well did I mix humanistic empathy, critical questioning, and comedic deftness today? instead of asking the more important question: How well did I help people learn today?

Focusing exclusively on exemplifying an idealized role model will condemn you to a pedagogic purgatory of unrealized aspirations. Since regularly achieving this perfectly balanced composite of admired behavior traits is impossible, you can easily become smitten by a sense of incurable guilt. You may crucify yourself on the cross of imagined perfectability and spend large parts of your educational life lamenting your having fallen short of an unrealizable ideal.

The kind of teaching teachers often feel they have to emulate is basically charismatic. Charismatic teachers are those dynamic performers we all know who can hold audiences in the palms of their hands and in whose presence students are enthralled and inspired. Brilliant performers like these often win Teacher of the Year awards, and it is easy to think that good teaching involves emulating these performers.

Yet many teachers are effective helpers of learning despite, or sometimes because of, their lack of flair for public performance. Some students are intimidated by charismatic teachers. Their exemplary command of their subjects and perfect demonstration of a set of skills, may lead these students to decide that their own abilities fall so pathetically short of these ideal states that there is little point in pursuing their learning any further. Yet these same students may react very well to teachers who are less comfortable as public performers and more attuned to working with small groups or individuals.

In and of itself, charismatic teaching is not in any way bad. The danger arises when this form of teaching is equated with the sum total of good practice. Remembering that charismatic teaching is but one of many teaching approaches and that, although it may work well with some people in some situations, other more individualized and relaxed approaches work just as well in others will help you keep your self-esteem intact when you don't win Teacher of the Year awards and when you fail to exhibit the perfect blend of characteristics you believe to be the hallmark of a good college teacher.

**Don't Confuse Academic Success with Teaching Skill.** There is a dangerous myth abroad that the best teachers are those who were the most successful as learners. According to this myth, someone with a degree from a prestigious university and an A+ average will be better equipped to teach a subject than someone with a B average and a degree from an underfinanced state college. This myth correlates intellectual achievement with pedagogic expertise, and it underlies the efforts to make teaching an all-graduate profession. It also underscores the system of incremental payments in some institutions whereby attaining a master's degree, and then a doctorate, results in the teacher moving one step up the pay scale. But in reality, those students who struggled in their own learning may be much better as teachers at understanding and assisting students who are struggling themselves.

It would obviously be foolish to advocate that teachers should be educational failures and to believe that a student's poor scores, failed exams, and frequent expulsions or periods of dropping out are somehow indicative of later pedagogic brilliance. But someone who has sailed through formal education with no perceptible effort, collecting A+ grades at every turn and graduating with honors, may find it particularly difficult to empathize with the anxieties and blockages experienced by some students. A good argument can be made that the teachers who display the most sensitivity to students' struggles, and who are the best equipped to help them work through these, are those who have themselves experienced similar struggles. So if you feel embarrassed about the pain and anxiety you experienced during your own academic studies, and if you tend to compare yourself unfavorably with colleagues who are academic successes, remember that your experiences may give you much greater insight into how your students deal with difficulties and how you can be of most help to them.

*Accept the Normality of Failure.* Failure is endemic to courageous, risk-taking teaching. One important indicator of good teaching is the readiness to take risks, particularly the risk of departing from the previously written "script" of an educational encounter to build on those "teachable" moments of energy and drama that arise unexpectedly in a class every so often. If you decide to take such risks, you must do so knowing that failure is a distinct possibility. Your apparently inspired divergence from carefully planned syllabuses and activities can sometimes backfire on you and lead to students feeling puzzled rather than excited and enlightened. So you need to recognize that failure is the normal accompaniment of a laudable readiness to experiment.

You must also avoid equating your finding yourself caught in the midst of seemingly intractable dilemmas with a failure to teach in an ordered, rational way. Teachers constantly face irritating and painful dilemmas. On a daily basis you probably face situations in which every course of action open to you leads to consequences you find unsatisfactory or unacceptable. All teachers regularly experience these dilemmas and feeling the pain they cause is a sign that you are critically alert to the consequences of your actions. It is when you stop hurting that you need to worry.

***Be Realistic About Your Limits.*** Finally, you need to develop a realistic attitude about the limits of what you can accomplish. The best teachers strive to implement their organizing visions while realizing that the imperfections of life mean this will never happen. They are fired by a passionate belief in the value of their work, but they are not thrown when students seem immune to this passion. We all want to effect significant change in all our learners and to have them view their interactions with us as life-transforming. We all want to teach in exactly the way we think is most effective and meaningful. But neither of these things is going to happen with great frequency. If you assess the value of your teaching by the extent to which they do, then you will eventually disappear under the weight of your accumulated sense of failure. To survive you need to know that social, economic, and political forces may severely limit the extent to which the sense of empowerment experienced inside classrooms can be exercised outside.

You also need to realize that teaching is often a series of

trade-offs. During a single class, let alone a single day, you'll need to choose among various options, all of which have drawbacks as well as benefits. No choice will be entirely advantageous. Someone (including you at times) will be unhappy with some aspects of your decision. So don't get into the habit of thinking that your choices must always be welcomed unequivocally by students or that you will feel totally satisfied with them. No matter how sensitively or diplomatically you approach your choices, someone is going to be angry or disappointed about the ones you make.

Living on the horns of irresolvable dilemmas is a fact of life for teachers. We have to weigh contradictory claims, try to project the consequences of our decisions, and know that no decision, however desirable, will be totally free of harmful effects. At some time or other we all have to ask ourselves questions such as, How much loyalty do I owe my employers and how much do I owe my students? How can I reconcile teaching what I feel is important with the contradictory demands expressed by students? How much time can I spend with one recalcitrant group member without endangering the learning of the majority? How can I judge when is a good time to risk departing from an educational plan and when I should stick to my outline? No matter how carefully you consider your answers to these questions, it is certain that at some points you'll have flashes of regret about them. You must always remind yourself that attending to your survival is not being thick-skinned or self-obsessed. It is the crucial emotional underpinning that allows you to experience the daily chaos of teaching in a way that celebrates rather than bemoans its diversity and unpredictability.

### Growing into the Truth of Teaching

I want to end this chapter with an affirmation. Despite its ambiguity, the experience of being a teacher is not one of total bewilderment and confusion. All of us over a period of time develop our own private truths about teaching. For me, this entire book represents what I feel to be the truth about teaching, but it has taken me twenty years to reach a point where I could declare this truth with some confidence. I regard much of my career as a process of growing into truth. By growing into truth I mean developing a trust—a sense of intuitive confidence—in the accuracy and validity of one's judgments and insights. This process doesn't involve an instantaneous conversion to a suddenly revealed reality, though moments of conversion sometimes do occur. Instead it is incremental and marked by a growing readiness to trust one's instincts even when these are contradicted by conventional wisdom and the pronouncements of authorities. Central to the process is the activity of "unlearning," that is, of weaning oneself away from an uncritical adherence to ideas and beliefs about teaching that are oversimplified, distorted by context, or just plain wrong.

Growing into truth takes time and courage. The judgments and insights we regard as true only become so by being tested and confirmed in the real-life contexts in which we work. If this truth contradicts what is declared by our colleagues, espoused within textbooks and journals, and enshrined in teacher-training programs, then admitting its validity to ourselves takes a great deal of courage. At first, the fact that your practice does not mirror the image of college teaching in teacher-training textbooks and programs can be explained away using two rationalizations. You can say to yourself that the principles and techniques of teaching that you've been taught are correct but that you're not yet adept enough at implementing them. Alternatively, you can say that your diversions from these principles and techniques are temporary and due to the distorting factors observable within the context in which you work.

At the beginning of my career, I used both these rationalizations, particularly the latter. But as time passed, and as it seemed that every context in which I worked contained factors that prevented the neat application of principles and techniques of "good" practice, I began to suspect that it was not the contexts that were wrong but the principles and techniques. Or rather not so much the principles and techniques themselves as my conviction that in order for me to be a proper teacher I had to apply them, relentlessly and rigidly, in every setting whether or not they seemed called for.

For twelve years I kept these suspicions buried. Only after I became a full-time university professor did I begin to admit them to myself. As I began to give keynote speeches and to conduct workshops and seminars (for now, as a professor, I was an "expert"), I began to air some of my suspicions and was astounded at the reaction. Again and again teachers attending workshops and conferences would come up to me and say, "I'm so glad you said what you did. I've always felt that there was something wrong with this or that approach to teaching but I've never felt that anyone else thought the same way. Hearing you talk about your own doubts was really exciting for me. It made me think that perhaps my ideas aren't as wrong as I thought."

Having my own insights confirmed by the experiences of so many practicing teachers was pleasing, but realizing that so many of them downplayed the significance of their own privately felt misgivings was discouraging. Many teachers dismiss their growing disquiet as evidence only of their inability to use methods correctly or to control their work contexts properly. Even when the clamor of their inner voices becomes too insistent to ignore, teachers may view their own concerns as irrational or irrelevant. These inner voices are only given serious attention when "experts" express these same concerns. Unfortunately we are sometimes so cowed by the presumed wisdom of authorities in our field that we think our own suspicions are of little consequence unless they are somehow legitimized by an expert (Cochran-Smith and Lytle, 1990).

I suspect that many teachers experience the process of growing into truth just as I did; that is, they come to trust their insights and judgments at the same time as they begin to decrease their dependence on decontextualized principles and techniques of good practice. The pace at which this happens is probably correlated with the variety of contexts in which teachers work. If you have worked for twenty years in

the same institution, you may believe that in a different context the principles and techniques of good practice will apply.
But when you change work settings and you find that each
new context exhibits a new set of idiosyncratic distortions,
you can no longer be so easily comforted by the thought that
it's the context that's wrong rather than your uncritical commitment to certain standardized approaches.

Until you begin to trust your inner voices, until you
accept the possibility that your instincts, intuitions, and
insights often possess as much validity of those of experts in
the field, and until you recognize that in the contexts in
which you work *you* are the expert, there is a real danger that
a profoundly debilitating sense of inadequacy may settle on
you. In the following chapters I hope that you will recognize
many of the situations I describe, the dilemmas I pose, and
the responses I suggest, and that as you read and reflect on
these you will find that the truth into which you have grown
is being increasingly confirmed.

# CHAPTER TWO

# Developing a Personal Vision of Teaching

As the previous chapter revealed, teachers describe the experience of teaching as complex, uncertain, and problematic. Given this situation, how can you as a teacher flourish in this maelstrom of ambiguity? How can you feel that amidst the unpredictable vicissitudes of classroom life your efforts mean something? One crucial response is for you to develop a critical rationale.

## Developing a Critical Rationale for Practice

A critical rationale is a set of values, beliefs, and convictions about the essential forms and fundamental purposes of teaching (Smyth, 1986). Embedded in this rationale are criteria for judging to what extent your practice exhibits features that you feel are essential to good teaching. At the center of a critical rationale is the distinctive set of aims towards which your efforts are geared (Eble, 1983). These aims and purposes provide an organizing vision of where you are going and why you are going there that you can present to students, and to yourself, with passion and clarity.

For a teacher in the classroom a critical rationale functions in much the same way as computerized navigation instruments do for air or sea pilots in the midst of a storm. Both devices help maintain a sense of stability and direction

even in the midst of foggy confusion. Calling upon a critical
rationale at times of crisis—such as your first encounter with
the unmanageability of teaching and learning—is one way to
keep your sense of yourself as a teacher intact. So developing
such a rationale to guide your practice is crucial for four
important domains of your life as a teacher: the personal, the
political, the professional, and the pedagogic.

The sustained experience of the chaotic ambiguity of
teaching—the feeling that things are not going as they should
and that unanticipated factors are distorting your painstak-
ingly prepared plans—can be extremely debilitating. At those
low points when you feel as though the insane (whether these
be learners, colleagues, or superiors) are in charge of the asy-
lum, you need to remind yourself of the reasons and purposes
that led you to teaching. It can be dangerous for you to feel
that in the storms of ambiguity through which you sail are
psychologically rudderless. It can be humiliating if others find
it easy to define your roles, aims, and functions for you. It can
be frustrating for you to realize that you have little sense of
why you're devoting enormous energies to your teaching.

With an organizing vision, you are less likely to suffer
from these feelings of uncertainty. A clear sense of purpose
helps you to endure periods of seemingly directionless confusion. During these periods you can resolve to conserve your
energies for the time when pursuing your vision is more possible. You can also think about how you might realize aspects
of your vision in smaller, more contained ways. So a distinctive organizing vision—a clear picture of why you're doing
what you're doing that you can call up at points of crisis—is
crucial to your personal sanity and morale.

Politically, such a rationale is also important. You will
sooner or later find yourself under pressure from powerful
figures in your institution to do things (such as introduce
poorly developed curricula, implement irrelevant evaluative
criteria, or adopt ineffective teaching methods) that you find
inappropriate and immoral. Sometimes there is little you can
do short of resigning. At other times, however, you can argue

against the wishes of institutionally powerful figures citing in your defense your distinctive organizing vision.

When combating pressures from above, it is enormously helpful to be able to express your opposition in terms of a confidently articulated rationale. You may or may not win your case or make your point. You will, however, be much more likely to communicate a sense of confident clearheadedness, a sense that your position is grounded in a well-developed and carefully conceived philosophy of practice. Opposition to the wishes of superiors that is self-evidently grounded in such a rationale is less likely to be interpreted as sheer personal stubbornness. You are more likely to gain a measure of respect for your thoughtfulness and commitment, which is important both for your self-esteem and for your political survival.

Professionally, a commitment to a shared rationale for college teaching is important for the development of a collective identity and, hence, for the development of professional strength among teachers. Most college teachers work within contexts that are clearly defined by the pursuit of particular curricular objectives. Ensconced comfortably within their familiar institutional or programmatic burrows, they rarely poke their noses out to sniff the wind blowing from other educational locations. In their belief that no one does exactly what they do, in precisely the manner in which they do it, they decide they have little in common with teachers in other settings or content areas. They claim to be teaching bodies of knowledge, particular skills, or required subject matter and declare that their only purpose is to develop these in students. They believe that more separates them from other teachers than unites them and that what they do has little impact beyond their particular educational enclaves.

If college teachers define themselves only as content or skill experts within some narrowly restricted domain, they effectively cut themselves off from some broader identity as change agents involved in helping students shape the world they inhabit. What is needed to counter this tendency towards isolated separatism is an underlying rationale for college teaching. This rationale, although it would acknowledge the importance of specialist curricula and expertise, would go beyond these to unite college teachers who work in very divergent contexts in the pursuit of shared purposes. I hope this book goes part way toward presenting a rationale that focuses on developing a sense of agency in students. This sense of agency—the inclination and capacity to create one's own values, meanings, and environment—is developed chiefly through the encouragement of critical thinking.

Finally, possessing a clear rationale for practice is, of course, pedagogically important. Knowing what the aims of your teaching are helps you to judge whether or not you are having the influence you would wish. It helps you immeasurably in evaluating your efforts if you have a clear idea of what you believe are the fundamental forms and purposes of college teaching. Since the aims of administrators and employers are often different from yours, it also reminds you that poor evaluations may mean nothing more than that others are judging your efforts by criteria that your rationale causes you to reject. Such evaluations hurt personally and politically and can be highly influential in determining whether you get or keep a job. So developing a clear rationale for practice— being able to say to yourself, "Well, even though no one else seems to understand why I'm doing what I'm doing, at least *I* know it's right for me and for my students, and I know why it's right"—is one important layer of the thick skin teachers need to protect themselves against the temporary debilitation of such evaluations.

Pedagogically, having a distinctive sense of why you are a teacher also means that you avoid the danger of being sidetracked into an exclusive concern with method. It can be easy to focus solely on whether or not you are demonstrating good process skills, however you might choose to define these. Important though these skills are, they are by no means the sum total of teaching. Teaching is about making some kind of dent in the world so that the world is different than it was before you practiced your craft. Knowing clearly what kind of dent you want to make in the world means that you must continually ask yourself the most fundamental evaluative question of all—What effect am I having on students and on their learning?

Asking this question also helps when you are faced with the need to choose between the conflicting claims and priorities advanced by superiors, colleagues, and learners. In such situations, it is important that you have some basis upon which to make your choice. Much of your energy as a teacher goes into finding partial resolutions to essentially irresolvable dilemmas. In your struggle to balance the risks and consequences of different actions, one of the most important things you must keep in mind is how the actions you are taking, and the choices you are making, connect to the overall aims you are pursuing.

If your teaching is grounded in a well-conceived rationale, you will also find that this has a powerful effect on your students. At times of uncertainty, they will draw strength from your passion and conviction. Students have the right to ask you to explain why you want them to do something. They may be worried that the content you propose to cover is irrelevant. They may feel that the learning methods you favor are entirely inappropriate or that the criteria applied to judging their efforts are unfair. In response to these legitimate concerns, you need to demonstrate to students that you know what you're doing. Even though many students may not agree with your explanations and justifications, they feel reassured when you can express these quickly, clearly, and confidently. They draw comfort from the fact that you, at least, seem to be quite sure that what's happening is valuable.

As Chapter Twelve shows, demonstrating that you have a carefully developed and deeply felt conviction about the importance of your teaching is an important element of the credibility students seek in their teachers. Showing that you know where you are going, and why you believe it's important to take students there with you, imbues the students with a sense of confidence. They realize they are under the guidance of someone who is experienced, insightful and, above

all, committed. When beginning a journey into unknown
and perilous intellectual and affective terrain—which is how
many people view learning—no one wants to feel that his or
her guide is inexperienced. It is disastrous for them to feel
either that you are unsure about the end point of the journey
or that you have doubts about whether it should be undertaken at all. Having a clear sense of where the journey is
leading and a deeply held belief in the importance of embark-
ing on it are attributes that come powerfully into play when
students feel lost, afraid, and confused along the way.

### A Rationale Proposed: Developing Critical Thinking

Throughout this book I propose the development of critical
thinking (Brookfield, 1987a) as the underlying rationale for
college teaching, providing both its method and its organizing vision. There are three reasons for making this argument.
First, critical thinking is one of the intellectual functions
most characteristic of adult life (Mezirow and Associates,
1990). Adulthood is the time when we begin to doubt the
universal truth or applicability of the tenets governing the
conduct of life that we learned in childhood or adolescence.
As we experience the dilemmas, ambiguities, and contradictions involved in trying to live in the adult world, we begin
to look critically at the accuracy and validity of these tenets.
We examine the fit between them and the contexts, choices,
and demands of adult life. Sometimes the fit is harmonious,
sometimes it is discordant. Since college students are on the
verge of, or fully immersed in, adult life, critical thinking
seems an entirely appropriate leitmotif for their education.
        Second, critical thinking is necessary for personal sur-
vival. It is a lived reality pressing in on us in the shifting
contexts of the personal, occupational, and political changes
we experience. It is not an abstract, academic exercise in arm-
chair philosophizing but an intellectual buoy that helps us
stay afloat on the tempestuous sea of change outside the
academy. As we try to make sense of our intimate relationships, we are emotionally disabled if we cannot interpret our

actions, and the rationales we cling to for justifying those actions, in a critical manner. In our workplaces the constantly changing patterns of organizational life and the chaotic unpredictability of the wider work world mean that being able to scrutinize the validity and accuracy of the assumptions upon which the workplace is based is crucial to survival. Organizations which presume that the assumptions and organizational mores that have worked comfortably for the last several decades are always going to serve them are heading for a brutal awakening.

Third, critical thinking is a political necessity in a democratic society. Educators from Dewey to Freire have considered the fostering of political literacy in students—the habits, knowledge, and inclinations needed to participate fully in democratic action—an important intellectual and philosophical element of higher education. An entirely appropriate aim of college teaching is to encourage students to develop a healthy attitude of critical scrutiny towards the actions and justifications of elected and unelected political leaders. The onset of the era of mass political advertising and the attempts by those running for political office to shield themselves from critical questioning with a barrage of pleasing images and jingles has made critical thinking even more crucial. Given that television is the chief source of political information for most people, an educational effort that helps them sift, filter, and critically decode the meanings and messages embedded within political commercials will also help nurture and maintain the democratic spirit (Brookfield, 1990a).

For these three reasons the development of critical thinking is an overarching aim of college teaching that crosses curricular contexts, educational settings, and the disciplinary identities with which teachers ally themselves (Meyers, 1986). Critical thinking is not a separate subject taught in a compartmentalized way. Instead, developing critical thinking is a process underlying all educational activities. Helping learners acquire a critically alert cast of mind—one that is skeptical of claims to final truths or ultimate solutions to problems, is open to alternatives, and acknowledges the contextuality of knowledge—is the quintessential educational process. It is as appropriate an aim for teachers of natural science and mathematics as it is for specialists in the humanities or social sciences.

Critically informed students of mathematics come to see forms of mathematical reasoning as elegant human constructs, not as divinely ordained universal patterns stumbled on by accident. Critically informed scientists come to see that the hypothetical-deductive method, accepted by many as the one method of reasoning in natural science, can be traced back to Francis Bacon's ideas. They also realize that what at one time might be seen as the divergent, unsubstantiated posturings of renegade mavericks outside the academy in later years often come to be regarded as major contributions to scientific understanding. They know that what are taken to be immutable physical laws of the universe change according to history and culture. Students learning craft skills begin to realize that the judgments informing what are "good" examples of their craft mirror dominant esthetic trends. They come to appreciate how good taste is a cultural construct, not an objective attribute. They are aware that generally accepted standards of excellence alter according to technological advances and to the changing dictates of fashion.

## Implementing Your Rationale Through Critically Responsive Teaching

Being clear about why you teach what you teach is crucial, but it is not enough in and of itself; you must also be able to communicate to your students the values, beliefs, and purposes comprising your rationale. You cannot assume that students will understand your rationale or be immediately convinced that your most deeply held convictions have a value for them as well. For example, in explaining what I think critical thinking is and why I feel it's important, I must leave behind the academic language and intellectual jargon with which I have grown familiar. I must find words, metaphors, and allusions that students recognize and comprehend. I must be ready to explain why students should take critical thinking seriously in terms that they appreciate, and are convinced by, rather than in my own terms.

It is not enough to say that people should be able to think critically because it's good for them. I cannot rely on their believing me when I say that being critically aware of the assumptions underlying our habitual ideas and actions is one important sign of maturity or one commonly accepted indicator of psychological development in adulthood. I must be willing to find out about students' backgrounds, cultures, outlooks, and expectations and, on the basis of this knowledge, find ways of communicating the importance of thinking critically that relate directly to these. Even if this means giving justifications for the importance of critical thinking that seem crass or overly utilitarian, I must suspend my prejudices and realize that unless I respond to students' concerns in ways they can appreciate, I stand little chance of convincing them.

Having a clear idea of what you wish to do, but being willing to adjust the means by which you think it best to do it, is a form of teaching that I describe as critically responsive teaching. Critically responsive teaching is teaching which is guided by a strongly felt rationale but which in its methods and forms responds creatively to the needs and concerns expressed by students. Guided as they are by deeply held convictions, critically responsive teachers nonetheless pay close attention to the ways in which students experience learning and to the myriad of contextual factors that no teacher can possibly anticipate.

The *critical* component of critically responsive teaching can be found in its concern to develop critical thinking. Critically responsive teachers help students to realize that dominant values, "commonsense" wisdoms, generally accepted standards, and prevailing social or political arrangements are cultural constructs. Because these are cultural creations, teachers point out that they can be dismantled and reframed by human agency. By creating this sense of agency in people, critically responsive teachers encourage the belief that the future is open, malleable, and waiting to be acted upon.

Critically responsive teaching aims to nurture in students a critically alert, questioning cast of mind. This cast of mind entails a readiness to scrutinize claims to universal truth with skepticism, to reject monocausal explanations of complex issues, and to mistrust final solutions to intractable problems. This critical skepticism challenges the belief that just because an idea, belief, social structure, or political arrangement has existed for a period of time it must, by definition, be correct. It is seen in a readiness to question the truth of an explanation that one is urged to accept solely because of the authority ascribed to its giver. Ultimately it involves a willingness to trust one's own experiences, insights, and intuitions as accurately representing reality even when these contradict dominant values and majority opinion. As the previous chapter showed, such a willingness is an important feature of the process of growing into truth.

The *responsive* component of critically responsive teaching is seen in the willingness of teachers to adapt their methods, content, and approaches to the contexts in which they are working and to the ways in which students are experiencing learning. Critically responsive teachers are not tied to some predetermined methodological stance. They are ready to mix small-group work with lectures, to alternate collaborative approaches with teacher-led projects, and to develop materials in cooperation with students as well as using standardized exercises. Responsiveness means that teachers judge whether or not to use a particular approach, method, or exercise by one criterion—whether or not it helps people learn. It means that they free themselves from the constraints of self-imposed dualistic paradigms governing their practice, such as humanism or behaviorism and banking or problem-posing education.

Let me give an example of responsiveness from my own practice. As a beginning college teacher, I was initiated into the espoused theory that discussion-based approaches were the most appropriate to working with college students. Lecturing, particularly, was viewed as domineering, authoritarian, and disrespectful of students' dignity. It was seen as emphasizing the power discrepancy between teacher and taught, it was held to prevent students becoming in any way involved in the educational process, and it was criticized for not taking account of students' experiences. If you lectured to students, so the conventional wisdom went, you were simply recreating the worst aspects of a discredited system of formal schooling. So, on entering college teaching I decided to run all my classes through discussion in the belief that this respected learners, involved them, and was admirably democratic. The fact that my own students sometimes disagreed with me on this was something I managed to deny or rationalize.

Yet, as time passed, many of the presuppositions I had uncritically accepted regarding the evils of lecturing and the benefits of discussion were contradicted by my experience. Students would plead for periods of lecturing. Discussions would be meandering and aimless. At times it was clearly evident that a laying out of ideas so that their interconnections could be seen was a useful prelude to focused discussion and to the critical thinking this encouraged. Students could not reflect critically upon a set of ideas or body of knowledge until they had had some relatively uncritical immersion in that content. People can only be critical in relation to something, whether this be a set of ideas, a collection of practices, or a social structure. However, because of my learned revulsion to lecturing I resisted using lectures as a means of providing the needed "something" students could first assimilate, reflect upon, and then explore critically. I denied the fact that a straightforward transmission of information through a lecture could be an important episode in an overall critical-thinking effort. In effect, I repeatedly ignored my own advice to judge whether or not to use a particular method by the extent to which it helps people learn.

When students protested that they wanted me to lecture more or that it was difficult for them to participate in the discussions we were having without a greater familiarity with the material (which could be quickly acquired with the aid of some lectures), I would assume, essentially, that I knew best. I interpreted their requests as merely indicative of the teacher dependency they had learned in school. I reasoned that if they felt discussions were meandering and aimless this was because they were not yet sophisticated enough at being discussion participants.

So my uncritical acceptance of the espoused idea that lecturing was disrespectful to learners blinded me to the reality that by refusing to lecture I was sometimes actively hindering their learning. I ignored the evidence of my own senses because I felt my pronouncements were of little validity when compared to those of experts in the field. When experts' pronouncements seemed to be contradicted by my own experiences, I concluded that this showed only that I had not fully understood these pronouncements. Basically, I denied my own inner voice and the voices of my students, refusing to trust either of these if they spoke against the disembodied voices of authorities as contained in textbooks. Far from indicating my respect for students, my refusal to lecture was actually a mark of disrespect.

As time passed, and as I became more confident that my own intuition was reliable, I began to lecture much more readily. I took seriously the students' opinion that it would be helpful for them if I lectured occasionally. I stopped denying the validity of students' experiences by always interpreting their requests for lectures as evidence of their immaturity, laziness, or inability to break their teacher dependency.

I told myself that sitting silently in a lecture hall paying close attention to teachers who are laying out a body of ideas is not to be equated with mental inertia. I knew listening to be a highly taxing activity, not a sign of passivity, and that interpreting someone else's comments, making sense of them within my own frame of reference, and tracing connections between these ideas and my experiences were activities that were intellectually demanding. I recalled that in my own intellectual development some of my most important insights occurred while I listened carefully to the comments of a provocative and critically stimulating presenter.

So gradually, at first with a frisson of secretive guilt, I introduced lectures into my teaching. From initially regarding this as something that must be kept private at all costs, I now happily admit to any who are interested that formal presentations take up between 20 to 25 percent of my total teaching time. Whereas years ago I would have regarded conference keynote speeches as purely ceremonial events with no intellectual significance (and many still are), I now believe that they can provoke valuable critical thought. I am very far from only using a lecturing approach, but I am much more inclined to mix periods of lecturing with large-group discussions, small-group exercises, and independent projects without regarding any of them as inherently more or less educational. In determining responsiveness in critically responsive teaching (as I did with my introduction of periods of lecturing), the crucial variables are context and experience. Do your methods and techniques help people learn in the context in which you and they are working? Do your approaches and exercises take account of how students are experiencing learning?

## A Final Note

An underlying rationale for practice, an organizing vision for teaching, critical thinking, critically responsive teaching—these perhaps seem abstract and remote philosophical concepts far removed from the exigencies of everyday practice. Nothing could be further from the truth. Even if you disagree profoundly with the rationale I am proposing (as many of you will), you cannot deny that being clear about why you are teaching is important to you and to those around you. It's not enough for you to accept whichever rationale your employers espouse at any particular time or to follow the pedagogic fashions of the moment. This might work for a while and you might even convince yourself, as well as your students and your colleagues, that your practice is grounded in strongly felt and carefully conceived convictions. But sooner or later your employers will change and pedagogic

fashions will alter. Then you'll realize that the convictions
you thought were solid are, in reality, opaque and insubstantial. This is a demoralizing insight and the alarm it induces
will soon spread to those around you.

So if you have forgotten what inspired you to become a
teacher in the first place, and if you can't recall why you felt
it was such an important way to spend your life, make a
deliberate and repeated effort to revisit the source of your
decisions and to drink from the waters there. On the other
hand, if you are one of those who fell into college teaching by
accident or if you had teaching responsibilities thrust upon
you, take the time to think long and hard about the values,
beliefs, and convictions by which you want your efforts to be
guided. The benefits to be gained from such reflection are
substantial. Your practice will be more focused. You will
imbue students with a sense of confidence in your abilities.
You will be respected by your colleagues. Most important of
all, perhaps, you will take seriously the effect that your teaching activities can have on your students' lives.

# CHAPTER THREE

# Teaching
Responsively

In the previous chapter I introduced the concept of critically responsive teaching and gave one example of responsiveness in my own practice. In the current chapter I take this theme of responsiveness further. In particular, I examine how you can make your teaching responsive by becoming aware of how students experience learning (Brookfield, 1990b). Having a clear appreciation of this is crucial for critically responsive teaching. To make choices about which methods and materials to use, how to pace educational activities, or what evaluative criteria are most accurate, you need hard evidence about how students perceive and respond to your actions.

There is no point adjusting your teaching to nonexistent concerns. There is no benefit in being responsive to situations or events you feel are important, if students do not share your sense of importance. It is all too easy to think you are working assiduously on students' behalf without actually ever asking whether they see your efforts in this way. And it is all too easy to miss points at which making adjustments would be enormously beneficial for students simply because you never found out how they felt about what was happening in the classroom.

In human communication the potential for mutual miscomprehension is ubiquitous, especially in the complex relationship between teachers and students. If you want to teach responsively, and if you want your adjustments, shifts, and changes to have something like the effects you intend, then you must first of all have as full an understanding as you can of how students experience learning. In Katz's (1985) phrase, you must teach as though students mattered.

## Researching Students' Experiences of Learning

As a critically responsive teacher, your practice exhibits a constant interplay between action and analysis. Although you are guided by a clearly defined organizing vision, you change your methods, content, and evaluative criteria as you come to know more about the ways these are perceived by students. Which knowledge and skills to explore next and how best to examine these are decisions made in the midst of the teaching activity itself, rather than being planned in detail from the outset. Thus regular discussions with students concerning how aspects of the educational process might be altered to make them more meaningful are an important aspect of such teaching. Negotiating and reframing sessions become familiar features of classroom life. Sometimes these sessions will lead to major shifts in direction or changes in method as you realize that your activities are not having the effect you hoped. At other times there will be little change, but students will have had the chance to question you about why you are doing what you are in the ways you are.

In order to teach responsively, you need to examine how students experience their learning. It is important to know what symbolic significance students ascribe to your actions. For the students, your choice of exercises, materials, and assignments evokes meanings you may not have intended. The ways you deal with students' criticisms of you, with their expressions of anger, or with their attempts to ingratiate themselves are watched very closely. I am continuously surprised by the variety of interpretations students make of some of my most incidental comments and the importance they give to offhand remarks.

It is also important to know something about the typical rhythms of learning. You want to discover the most commonly experienced peaks and troughs, the events students remember as alienating and those they remember as affirming, and why this is so. It is helpful to get a sense of how they experience learning something new and difficult and what helps reduce the anxiety aroused by confronting unfamiliar activities or ideas. Knowing how they react to criticism, how they deal with failure, and how they move out of a frustrating period of being stalled or blocked is crucial to your practice. If you have some insight into these rhythms you can compensate for periods that are too frantic and you can move more quickly through periods that seem lethargic. You can anticipate periods of frustration and anxiety and know what signs to look for when these occur. You are better placed to withstand the expressions of anger and resentment that accompany frustration and you can forestall some of these by removing unnecessary blockages.

How can you do this? Four sources are of particular importance: (1) students' descriptions of the most critical incidents in their learning, (2) learning journals describing the intellectual and emotional terrain of students' journeys, (3) documented accounts of the experience of learning compiled by researchers, and (4) teachers' reflections on their own biographies as learners. Let me say something about each of these sources.

*Critical Incidents.* Critical incidents (Brookfield, 1990c) are brief written reports compiled by students about their experience of learning. These reports describe events that are recalled vividly and easily because of their particular significance for students. They stand out in sharp relief from the canvas of their experience. In workshops on faculty development, teaching, and learning over the years, I have often used a critical incident questionnaire to show teachers how they can become aware of how their students experience learning. This instrument can be easily adapted by teachers in a variety of contexts; it is reproduced below. It contains a series of questions that are deliberately framed to elicit descriptions of specific events, rather than asking for general observations about the nature of teaching. As such they have the great advantage of being relatively easy to answer, and hence of not threatening or intimidating students yet still producing highly revealing responses.

*Critical Incident Questionnaire: Experiencing Learning*

Think back over the last experience you had as a learner participating in a planned educational program (such as a course, workshop, or conference). Describe, in as specific, concrete, and honest a fashion as you can, the following details of this experience:

1.  The incident (or incidents) that you recall as being the most exciting and rewarding because it represented a learning "high" for you—a time when you felt that something important and significant was happening to you as a learner.
2.  The incident (or incidents) that you recall as being the most distressing or disappointing for you because it represented a learning "low"—a time when you felt despair or frustration about your learning activities.
3.  The characteristics and behaviors of teachers that you found most helpful to your learning. Give specific examples of events in which these were observable.
4.  The characteristics and behaviors of teachers that you found hindered your learning. Give specific examples of events in which these were observable.
5.  Those times when you felt valued and affirmed as a learner and why this was so.
6.  Those times when you felt demeaned and patronized as a learner and why this was so.
7.  The most important insights you realized about the nature of effective teaching.
8.  The most important insights you realized about yourself as a learner.
9.  The most pleasurable aspects of learning you experienced.
10. The most painful aspects of learning you experienced.

Now, review the responses you've given to these ten questions and analyze these with regard to the following themes:

1. What common themes emerge from your descriptions of the learning experiences that are most useful to you?
2. What common themes emerge from your descriptions of the learning experiences that are least useful to you?
3. What advice would you give to a new learner concerning how to survive and succeed within formal education?
4. What advice would you give to a teacher concerning methods and behaviors that would be most helpful to learners?

Here is another, much shorter, form of critical incident exercise you might try.

### Critical Incident Exercise: Confidence in Learning

Think back over your last six months as a learner. At what point did you first feel confident enough to write or speak an opinion that you knew contradicted the expert wisdom in your subject. Write a brief description of when this happened (no more than one page). Make sure you describe in detail where and when this occurred, who was involved (please use job titles and functions here, not names) and what it was that you think gave you the confidence to challenge the "experts."

Or, you may want to use something like the following:

### Critical Incident Exercise: Hitting Bottom

Think back to the last time when you felt ready to give up trying to learn a particular skill, subject, concept, or piece of knowledge—a time when you hit bottom and said to yourself, "Things can't get any worse than this." Why did you keep on learning? What was it that stopped you giving up completely? Write down whatever you remember about the factor or factors that helped you through this low period in your life as a learner.

As a teacher you will mostly be concerned to interpret the information provided in responses to these critical incident exercises in terms of its effect on your practice. But being aware of the patterns and processes of their own learning and of which teaching behaviors are helpful and which harmful is just as useful for students. Helping students develop some awareness of their preferred learning styles—of their habitual ways of acquiring knowledge, developing skills, and realizing insights—is one of the most significant things teachers can do for students.

Reflecting on their educational experiences helps students understand and take control over this crucial aspect of their lives. It means they can be initiators rather than reactors. They can choose approaches and teaching personalities they find most congenial. They can learn how to anticipate and adjust for their most obvious weaknesses. They are better placed to prepare themselves for the inevitable periods of pain and anxiety that are endemic to learning. And they are more likely to be able to free themselves from tendencies and inclinations that may be perceived as natural and comfortable in the short run, but that are really self-defeating in the long run.

*Learning Journals.* Learning journals (Modra, 1989; Lukinsky, 1990) are private records of how students feel about and make sense of their learning. They provide a direct and immediate recounting of learners' experiences that are relatively undistorted by teacher or researcher interventions. Provided that instructions for keeping journals are clear and simple and avoid phenomenological jargon, students should not find it too onerous or time-consuming to maintain a brief, but highly informative journal. As an example of what a learning journal could contain, you might want to ask students to jot down their responses to the following questions at the end of each class.

*Learning Journal Instructions*

Think back over the class and note down the following details:

1.  The activity that gave you the most intense learning "high." What was it about this activity that was so exciting or pleasing?
2.  The time in the class when you felt most valued and affirmed and why you think this was so.
3.  The activity that gave you the most intense learning "low." What was it about this activity that was so distressing or hurtful?
4.  The time in the class when you felt most demeaned and patronized and why you think this was so.
5.  The most important insight you realized in the class about your own emotional responses and learning processes.

After students have assembled a collection of journal entries written after each class session, it is fascinating for them, and for you, to look for patterns, rhythms, and regularities. You can begin to discover how your actions as a teacher are perceived and what activities and materials are meaningful to which students. Although the responses to the five questions outlined above take very little time to complete after each session, the insights they can yield, especially when journals that have been compiled over time are read in sequence, should be taken seriously. In contrast to critical incident responses, which are cross-sectional snapshots of vividly remembered highs or lows, learning journals provide a longitudinal perspective on the experience of learning.

When you read students' journals, their contents must be kept in confidence and not shared with other students unless the writers first agree, and even then the identities of the writers should be disguised. You can't assume, of course, that the perceptions revealed in learning journals are impartial and comprehensive. Journals are records of individual perceptions, not objective depictions of reality. Learners may represent themselves in a better light in their journal entries than was the case in actuality, or they may show very little understanding of their own learning processes. Not all students are immediately comfortable with keeping learning journals nor are they sophisticated in doing so. But if you can encourage students to get into the habit of writing brief journal entries they, and you, can learn a great deal from regularly reviewing these.

*Studies of How Students Experience Learning.* In recent years there has been a growing interest among many educational researchers in recording learners' direct perceptions of their learning experiences (Entwhistle and Ramsden, 1983; Marton, Hounsell, and Entwhistle, 1984). As a concept, experiential learning (Kolb, 1984) has become an accepted part of the educational lexicon, and this has focused attention on the affective as well as the cognitive aspects of learning. Many researchers have decided that it is just as important to study learning from the learner's viewpoint as it is to study how teachers view their students' learning. Three important anthologies, *Reflection* (Boud, Keogh, and Walker, 1985), *Appreciating Adults Learning* (Boud and Griffin, 1987), and *Developing Student Autonomy in Learning* (Boud, 1988), contain descriptions of learning episodes from the learners' perspective.

A number of dissertations at the Ontario Institute for Studies in Education have explored this same theme in a variety of educational contexts (Bates, 1979; Denis, 1979; Taylor, 1979; Boyd, 1981; Griffith, 1982; Gehrels, 1984; Robinson, Saberton, and Griffin, 1985; D'Andrea, 1985; Barer-Stein, 1985). Then there are studies of women's experience of college learning (Mezirow, 1977; Maclaren, 1986; Belenky, Clinchy, Goldberger, and Tarule, 1986; Persico, 1988; Hutchinson and Hutchinson, 1988; Tarule, 1988; Butterwick, 1988; Rannells Saul, 1989), of college students' "best" and "worst" classroom learning experiences (Sheckley, 1988), and of students' perceptions of teachers' actions (Conti and Fellenz, 1988; Ross and Pena, 1988). There are also cross-cultural analyses of learners' perceptions of learning (Pratt, 1988a, 1989) and works exploring the experiences of students in a "Second Chance" program for working-class adults (Edwards, 1986), literacy students' views of success and failure (Charnley and Jones, 1979; Van Tilburg and DuBois, 1989), the experience of learning of adult university students (Elsey, 1982; Woodley and others, 1987; Grossman, 1988; Chene, 1988), students' perceptions of teachers' attempts to negotiate curricula with them (Millar, Morphett, and Saddington, 1987), the experience of learning within "open" learning systems (Coggins, 1988; Graff and Coggins, 1989), and how the activities of self-directed learners contradict conventional wisdoms about many learning processes (Brookfield, 1981; Danis and Tremblay, 1988; Spear and Mocker, 1984; Spear, 1988). The number of learners featured in these studies runs into the thousands, so reviewing these provides a reasonably solid (though highly ethnocentric) empirical basis for generalizations about the experience of learning. Some of the most interesting insights revealed in these studies are summarized in the next chapter.

*Teachers' Biographies as Learners.* One of the best ways you can gain insight into the experience of learning is to study your own learning. Most teachers, as participants in staff development activities, professional development workshops, or graduate study, are themselves learners. Participating in formal educational activities provides a rich source of insights regarding how it feels to be a learner. If any of your life is spent as a learner you can use this experience to great effect. You can try to identify turning points in your own transformations and think about the exercises or teaching actions that prompted these. You can explore which factors were influential when you surprised yourself by deciding to try to learn something you had always avoided up to that point. You can think about the times you felt affirmed and respected as a learner, and about the times you felt humiliated, and try to pinpoint what caused those feelings. You can review the evaluations you received that left you debilitated and depressed, and those that you found helpful, and try to work out what it was that was so different about these.

Reflecting on all these features of your learning experience has powerful implications for your own teaching. It will make you much more aware of the effects your actions are having on learners. If you have just been destroyed by a tactless criticism from your doctoral adviser you will be less likely to be so tactless in evaluating your own students. If you were helped through an intimidating staff development activity by your leader's clearly given instructions and regular encouragement, you will be reminded of the importance of these for your own students.

It is also interesting to analyze how far your own, privately developed, informal theories of teaching spring from your experiences as a learner. You may well find that the rules of thumb, insights, hunches, and values you have evolved to guide your practice are derived from those episodes, as a learner, in which your concerns and passions were most deeply felt. In my case, the teachers and teaching I regard as exemplary, the research areas I have chosen to explore, and the philosophical traditions with which I ally myself are directly connected to my perceptions of how it feels to be a learner. In particular, those instances in which I was institutionally defined as having failed have been pivotal to my teaching.

At age eighteen I was turned down for university study having failed to achieve the necessary grades in my preuniversity examinations. As an undergraduate at a British polytechnic (that did not require such high grades for admission), I earned a highly unremarkable "lower second" honors degree—in American terms something like having a B or B-average. In my master's degree examinations, my performance was judged "borderline," which meant that my graduation depended on the thesis I wrote without sustained advice (I did graduate). Up to this time, my biography as a learner was one of struggle, boredom, and unremarkable performance as measured by a succession of standardized examinations. It was dazzling in its mediocrity.

Something happened, however, when I entered graduate study in adult education. I was encouraged to define my own learning projects, treated by professors as a colleague, asked to analyze my own experience as a learner and teacher, and expected to conduct critical appraisals of my own work rather than relying solely on professors for these evaluations.

Not only did I find this personally congenial, but my performance (in institutionally defined terms) immediately improved.

As I reflect on my own beliefs about teaching, I realize that many of them grow out of my own excitement and frustration as a learner. My emphasis on teachers modeling the behavior they expect in students, my encouragement of critical thinking, my suspicion of standardized teaching approaches, and my insistence on teachers' words and actions being congruent all derive from my experiences as a learner, especially from those times when I suffered from uncritical and self-important teachers, from mindless pedagogic fads, and from blatant (but unchallenged) contradictions between what teachers said they believed in and what they actually did.

Acknowledging the biographical basis to teaching and allowing your perceptions of your own learning to guide aspects of your teaching will inevitably open you to the criticism that your practice is subjectively based (which, to some extent, is true of all practice) and that in this subjectivity lies a major weakness. How, your critics will ask, can an approach to teaching based partly on personal experience have any general usefulness? This is a legitimate criticism. In response we must look to the tradition of phenomenological inquiry and in particular to its contention that aspects of generic processes are evident in single acts.

The phenomenological truth of an insight does not depend on the number of people who report its occurrence. Aspects of many teachers' experiences can be embedded in one teacher's actions. One person's formulation of a problem, or exploration of a dilemma, may contain many points of connection to others' experiences. For example, my experiences dealing with overly domineering or passive group members or with trying to balance my own convictions about what students need with the needs that they express themselves may, in one sense, be completely unique to me. But there will also be some elements in my personal experiences that others will recognize. In my formulation of, and response to, these problems or dilemmas there will be parallels with many other teachers' experiences.

However, relying solely on your own experience as a learner to guide your teaching can be risky. Because of some unusual incident in your history, you may emphasize a teaching approach that is inappropriate to the context in which you work. Thus, although you should certainly reflect upon your own experience as a learner, you should also try to guard against making your teaching responsive to distorted aspects of your own experience. You can do this by using critical incidents and learning journals to enter the phenomenological worlds of the learners you work with, and by consulting other accounts of students' experiences of learning that have been compiled by researchers.

## Experiencing Learning as an Approach to Faculty Development

In many teaching institutions a great deal of time and money is devoted to various professional development and in-service education activities designed to improve practice (Weimer, 1990). Often highly paid consultants are brought in to tell teachers what their problems are and to solve these for them. These faculty development efforts are often useful, and there are many contributions that outsiders can make to helping teachers improve their practice. As someone who is often asked to visit institutions for a day or two to work with teachers, I know that I can ask questions and make observations that are politically dangerous for junior teachers to raise. I can ask the questions that are so obvious to an outsider but that elude those caught within the distorted perspectives of a situation. I can try to prompt teachers to critically reconsider assumptions that frame how they perceive and practice their craft. I can introduce teachers to concepts, models, insights, and practices that somehow connect to their own contexts and that might help them to clarify what were previously seen as inextricable complications.

But another approach to faculty development is just as valuable (and often far simpler and cheaper). Unfortunately, it has generally been neglected. This approach is, quite simply, to ask teachers to experience learning (Woods and Sykes, 1987). In particular, to ask them to try to learn something new and difficult, to reflect on how this feels, and then to interpret what this means for their own teaching. In the first stage of this process, teachers are released from part of their normal duties to learn something that is unfamiliar and intimidating to them. As they experience this process they recognize their emotional peaks and troughs. They note those times they feel threatened and those times they feel exhilarated. They identify those teacher actions that encourage and affirm them and those that intimidate and infantilize them. They observe what enhances their learning and what hinders it.

As teachers reflect on these experiences, they begin to see implications for their own teaching practices. They think about the symbolic significance to students of their own actions as teachers. They note the aspects of their own practice that inhibit, intimidate, and infantilize students and try to reduce them. They work to incorporate the approaches and behaviors that most assisted their own learning.

This process of reflective analysis is undertaken concurrently with learning, and it occurs both individually and in groups. Teachers keep journals (Holly, 1987; Tripp, 1987) in which they note down critical episodes and events in their learning and record the actions and processes that enhance or hinder this. They meet with other teachers from the same institution who are experiencing the same process of learning something new and unfamiliar but in a range of different contexts. In comparing vividly remembered episodes, insulting or affirming teacher actions, or methods and exercises that worked especially well, they gain insight into which features of teaching hold true across settings and which are specific to a certain context.

## The Benefits of Teaching Responsively

Teaching responsively is neither easy nor convenient, and it runs against many organizational assumptions. It means that you cannot plan objectives and methods or predict exact outcomes months in advance. You cannot fix evaluative criteria at the start of an educational activity and expect these to be as relevant at the end as they were at the beginning. Being responsive to students' experiences of learning makes your assessments of your effectiveness as a teacher at least partly dependent on students' perceptions of what is happening to them. Such contextual notions of effectiveness do not always sit well with the administrative desire to standardize effectiveness through a series of easily replicable indicators.

So trying to understand how students experience learning, analyzing your practice to see how you can take account of this understanding, and reframing your purposes, methods, and evaluative criteria as dominant themes or concerns emerge from your students is complex, ambiguous, and institutionally inconvenient. But, although the effort required is substantial, so are the rewards. At the very least you will be alerted to common rhythms of learning and to crucial turning points. You will be less likely to make some of the more frequent mistakes that arise when teachers underestimate the complexity of learning. You will develop a healthy skepticism about standardized curricula, packaged materials, and centrally prescribed evaluative criteria. Most important of all, perhaps, you will cease pursuing the chimera of the one method of college teaching that is suitable to all contexts, purposes, and students.

# CHAPTER FOUR

# Understanding the Tensions and Emotions of Learning

The published studies mentioned in the previous chapter describe the learning experiences of thousands of students. Despite this seemingly large number of students, the insights presented after reviewing these reports are tentative and provisional. They are also extremely ethnocentric, representing as they do experiences of students in the English-speaking world. Students in formal educational programs in the United States, Canada, Britain, New Zealand, and Australia (the five countries reviewed in these sources) must not be considered representative of the larger populations of these societies, let alone the world.

But although these studies may not allow us to construct a fully comprehensive theory of learning, the insights these studies provide are important for two reasons. First, on a practical level, they support much of the advice given throughout this book on the practice of teaching. Second, they are certainly more grounded in the reality of learning as experienced across contexts and cultures than are some of the personal prescriptions contained in teaching textbooks. But don't think that these insights capture the "truth" about learning or that if some of these features are missing from your own practice something must be wrong with your practice.

With these caveats in place, let me now discuss the most interesting elements of the experience of learning and those

43

that seem to have the greatest replicability across the varied cultures and contexts in which these experiences are reported.

## The Impostor Syndrome

From basic education students to students in doctoral programs, there is a very commonly reported perception of impostorship. Students within formal education say that they should not really be there, that they are somehow impostors. They report how, at the beginning of a new course or program, they wrestle with deciding whether or not to continue when they see how capable all the other students are. When they contrast what they see as their own poor abilities with what they regard as the sophistication of their peers, they wonder if perhaps a mistake has been made. They wonder if an administrator has confused their file with that of another student or if their name was erroneously entered on the "accept" list instead of on the "reject" one.

Ironically a great number of new students believe they have entered a program under false pretenses and perceive everyone else as being much more capable and confident than themselves. This feeling of being undeserving impostors who will sooner or later have their real, pathetically inadequate identities revealed is remarkably consistent across contexts. In my own practice I had expected such levels of poor self-regard from students stereotypically labeled as "disadvantaged," such as those in literacy or remedial education programs. It has been a revelation to encounter such feelings among many doctoral students and among participants in professional development workshops, many of whom are senior professionals occupying positions of great power and teaching responsibility in their work lives.

A strong element of authority dependence seems to pervade many people's educational socialization, and this dependence predisposes them to regress to childlike behavior upon entering a classroom or formal educational setting. People returning to formal education after a period away should not be thought of as supremely confident, self-directed learners who are anxious to escape the confines of teacher and institutionally imposed constraints. In actuality, many of them yearn for these confining constraints. They think that they can keep their impostorship secret by seizing on cues tossed off by teachers about what behaviors are expected.

What strikes me about this impostor syndrome is how closely it parallels my own experience, not only as a learner, but also as a supposed "expert" on adult learning and education. Whenever I am asked to address a group of practitioners or to give a speech at a conference, I ask myself what I can possibly offer that can have any relevance or use to such people. The teachers I meet at such gatherings seem to have such a wealth of experience and to be working in such insightful and innovative ways that I doubt whether anything I say will have any meaning or validity for them. I feel, in fact, like an impostor who, as soon as he starts speaking, will send the people who arranged his visit into paroxysms of embarrassment at their lapse of judgment.

The fact that this has never happened (or if it does, that people hide it from me) doesn't seem to have diminished the strength of this feeling. This reaction can, of course, be interpreted as grandiose self-importance masked as an appealing modesty. But from my conversations with teachers over the years, I believe that many teachers experience the imposter syndrome at various times. Just think back to the last time you had to give a formal presentation at a professional conference. It would not be at all surprising if you recall feeling the same sense of impostorship at presuming to address your peers that your students feel when they compare themselves to their peers.

### Emotionality

When students speak about learning, they do so in highly emotional terms. This isn't surprising, yet the emotional dimensions of learning receive scant attention in formal research, for they escape standardized measures and experimental controls. As a researcher, it is much easier to focus on how learners perform according to unequivocally defined measures of achievement than it is to explore the discordant intensity of learners' emotional reactions. To students, however, their feelings and emotions run the gamut from profound embarrassment at their inability to seem as assured and confident as they feel they ought, to deep, angry resentment at the dismissive arrogance sometimes displayed by teachers. More positively, they feel aroused and excited at the prospect of being able to break out of conventionally accepted ways of thinking and behaving, and they are exhilarated when they can perform difficult tasks or understand complex ideas.

When experiencing learning, students speak of stumbling across an insight or making an important connection in very physiological terms. They speak about getting chills, about their hair standing up on the back of their necks, or about their pulse racing with excitement. They talk about feeling flushed with anger or hot with embarrassment, or they describe a painful knot of anxiety forming inside their stomachs as they see themselves falling short of self-imposed or teacher-prescribed standards. Learning is rarely experienced in an emotionally denuded, anodyne way. This is in contrast to teaching, which is often spoken of by students as exhaustingly, mind-numbingly boring. Evidently the activity of teachers teaching often has little to do with learners learning.

One of the most common emotional reactions reported by students, particularly where significant change is occurring, concerns a grieving for lost certainties. In critical-thinking episodes or educational experiences described as "transformative," there are times when what was thought to be fixed, true, and permanent is found to be relative, shifting, and culturally specific. When people question the assumptions underlying habitually accepted ideas or actions, they end this process by discarding some of these. What were previously accepted as commonsense, taken-for-granted, conventional wisdoms are now seen as distorted and inadequate to account for reality.

This process is not entirely joyful, in fact it is often distressing and disturbing. Consequently, there is often a wistful looking back to what is seen as an age of innocence existing before the learning episode. This age is viewed as a time of fixed certainties, of dualistic distinctions between right and wrong, good and bad. When an educational event causes students to question habitual assumptions it unsettles their comfortable worldviews. The world becomes seen as malleable rather than set in place, as humanly constructed rather than divinely ordained.

Teachers often make the mistake of presuming that this realization of the contingency of ideas, behaviors, and structures will be experienced by students as liberating and exciting. They expect that students who see themselves freed from the shackles of distorted perspectives and invalid assumptions will feel a sense of release or gratitude towards the teacher who has made this transformative breakthrough possible. This is certainly one element frequently found in students' emotional reactions to discarding past assumptions, but it is not its sum total. Realizing the erroneous nature of past assumptions can remove from people some of the comfortable rationalizations they could use to justify their habitual behaviors and ideas. Because of the discomfort this causes, students will often resent the teacher who has jerked them rudely out of a golden era of certainty.

If teachers are not aware of the strong possibility that students may be angry and resentful, they may feel very threatened when this occurs. Under this sense of threat, they may feel that they have failed in their educational efforts. Knowing that these emotional reactions are typical helps teachers live through them. They can anticipate students' annoyance at having had the rug woven of unquestioned assumptions, fixed dualities, and universal truths pulled out from under them.

Being aware of the possibility of anger also stops teachers from rushing prematurely to quell this. One unfortunate tendency of many teachers is to feel that displays of emotion are inappropriate in classrooms. They view a student's expression of anger or resentment as an "outburst"—a volcanic eruption of disruptive passion that must be capped

as quickly as possible before other students are burned by the
heat of this emotional lava. But learning, and teaching, are
passionate, emotional activities. To devote yourself to keeping
classrooms free from the messiness of emotions is to deny
much of the power of learning and teaching.

This is why, over the years, I have become less inhibited
about showing how learners' positive reactions to my teaching (when they have occurred!) have affected me. Instead of
desperately trying to control my lower lip, diving for my hand-
kerchief in a pretence that I have suddenly caught hay fever,
and straining to keep my eyes as dry as a bone, I have become
much more ready to let students see the powerful effects their
expressions of appreciation have had upon me. I don't want
to suggest that I sob my way histrionically through positive
evaluations of my practice. But I do think that allowing students to see that teaching is infused with emotion and passion
for me sends a message that their feeling emotional about
their own learning is something to be expected.

### Challenge

When asked to speak about significant learning episodes—
those that are vividly remembered as being crucially transformative and that are spoken about with pride—it is interesting how many students speak of episodes in which
challenge was a central feature. They will choose events and
occasions when they were faced with difficult situations or
with dilemmas that had no clear resolution. These might be
situations in which they were required to explore areas of
knowledge that they found intimidating, times when they
had to learn new skills that did not come easily to them, or
occasions when they were asked to explore a worldview or
interpretive frame of reference with which they did not feel
comfortable. During these challenging episodes, students feel
exposed and at risk.

The sense of risk and exposure heightens the significance these episodes hold for students so that these episodes
become transformative turning points leading to changes in

students' self-concepts. What is recalled with satisfaction is the way in which the challenge was faced and dealt with so that students felt they had satisfactorily managed a problematic situation. This experience of grappling successfully with what was initially threatening is truly empowering. Areas that students previously considered out of bounds are reinterpreted as being within their purview. So confronting a challenge is often a marker event in students' development.

As can be appreciated, the emotional tenor of these episodes is complex. As students recall them, they speak of the threats to the ego entailed in exploring problematic areas of knowledge, new skills, or unfamiliar interpretive frameworks. Yet the newly revealed capacity to successfully complete these explorations is remembered with pride. An important aspect is the exhilaratingly liberating feeling of having survived experiences that had previously been perceived as terrifying and as totally beyond one's capacity.

Students talk about passing statistics exams, writing philosophy papers, confronting authority figures such as professors, giving a spoken presentation in front of a group of peers, or defending a thesis to a hostile committee as events that, in anticipation, have reduced them to states of fearful incoherence. Nothing—not their previous accomplishments, not the positions of responsibility they assume outside their student role, not the assurances they receive from teachers that everyone else survives these events—seems to reduce their anxiety. But, after not only surviving but flourishing in these situations, students experience a leap in self-confidence, a sense that, "Well, if I can do this here, then maybe that other area I've always been so frightened of isn't going to be so difficult after all."

One final point. Sometimes the events that so threaten students are ones that teachers regard as fairly routine. If you have been teaching the same subject, in the same way, for a period of time, it is easy to find your emotional senses dulled. Unless you yourself have had to learn something difficult recently (a staff development practice I heartily endorse) you are likely to have forgotten how this can turn your bowels to water and your legs to jelly. So remember that what to you as a teacher might appear as an accomplishment of very little significance—such as a novice computer student writing a letter using a word processor, a literacy student writing the name of a favorite baseball team, or a nonswimmer spluttering down the swimming pool to touch the tiling at the end for the first time—might be experienced by the students involved as breakthrough transformations.

## Reflection

One of the most frequently espoused principles of skillful teaching is that of praxis, that is, of ensuring that opportunities for the interplay between action and reflection are available in a balanced way for students. Praxis means that curricula are not studied in some kind of artificial isolation, but that ideas, skills, and insights learned in a classroom are tested and experienced in real life. Essential to praxis is the opportunity to reflect on experience, so that formal study is informed by some appreciation of reality. Although the apparent division between action and reflection in praxis is conceptually clean, it is not paralleled in actuality. Schön's (1983) work on reflection in action is especially interesting because it describes how practitioners reflect on events while "inside" them.

Despite the frequency with which teachers espouse the principle of praxis, however, in reality it seems that the active component is given far more emphasis than the reflective. Students typically say that teachers rush through masses of content and that assignments designed to assess students' familiarity with this content come so thick and fast that there is barely time to assimilate new ideas and knowledge, let alone to reflect on these. There is apparently little chance for students to interpret what they are being exposed to in terms of their past experiences or to trace connections between new ideas and perspectives and their already evolved structures of understanding. The period for mulling over that is reportedly needed for learners to make interpretive sense of what is happening to them is neglected.

In terms of models of experiential learning, the cycle of concrete experience, reflection on that experience, abstract conceptualization, and application of insights in new contexts is broken by learners not experiencing fully the reflective observation or abstract conceptualization components. One of students' most frequently expressed lamentations after finishing a course or program is that the richness of the experience was reduced so drastically by their being forced to do too much in too short a time. They speak of information overload or of the danger of exploding from the amount of knowledge crammed into them.

Teachers seem to err in favor of breadth over depth when covering new content, or, if they favor depth, they dive too deep too quickly. In effect, students suffer "the bends" induced by being forced to go deeper into a subject than their preparation allows. Teachers' tendency to overestimate the amount and intensity of learning their students can take is usually due to a combination of factors. Sometimes teachers' own familiarity with an area dulls them to the complexities that its study represents for students. Sometimes they are constrained to meet the requirements of accrediting or licensing bodies. Sometimes there is the institutionally prescribed need to fit students into a series of courses so that they can keep up with the other components of a program of study.

Whatever the reasons, the emphasis on breadth in particular leaves students feeling that they have never really come to grips with a new knowledge or skill area. They say that they have never learned the "grammar" of the activity they are exploring. They complain about never having learned the basic internal criteria, organizing concepts, and broad categorizations prevalent in the bodies of knowledge or skill sets they are studying.

These comments do not come from lazy students carping unreasonably about the perfectly fair requirements of conscientious teachers. They are expressed with a sense of regret that what could have been such a connected, meaningful experience was rendered so fleeting and unsatisfactory by the lack of opportunity for reflection on what was being learned. Students intuitively sense that reflection and action need to be balanced for them to make the most of their learning; when the reflective component is neglected, they experience a marked diminution in its richness.

Students also report an overemphasis by teachers on the action component of praxis with respect to teaching methods. They speak of endless small-group exercises that are conducted because the teacher feels that they are somehow expected but that serve no clearly discernible purpose. Far from increasing the intensity, connectedness, and richness of the educational event small-group work is often perceived as meaningless busy work. It is sometimes interpreted as a sign of a teacher's laziness, disinterest, lack of expertise, or insecurity. The inference is often made that frequent use of small-group methods indicates nothing so much as a teacher's refusal to do the necessary preparation for proper teaching.

### Incremental Fluctuation

Students often speak of moving through significant learning episodes in terms that suggest incremental fluctuation. This is particularly so with critical thinking (Brookfield, 1987a), but I venture that it holds true for other domains as well. In learning critical thinking, people make explicit some assumptions on which their habitual ways of thinking and acting have been based and then begin to discard some of these assumptions and to reframe others to fit their experience of reality. This process is seldom experienced sequentially in a neat developmental fashion (the way that many curricula are organized). More frequently it is reported as a case of "two steps forward, one step back"—a kind of transitional mambo.

Frequently, an initial sense of release and liberation invigorates a student who is exploring a new area of knowledge, trying out a new skill, or examining alternative perspectives. What follows this initial enthusiasm is often anxiety about the unfamiliarity of these new ways of thinking and acting and a concurrent longing for the security of old ideas and behaviors. Feeling this way, students retreat to their familiar, and recently discarded, assumptions and habits with the sense of having "come home." They are warmed by the comfortable reassurance of the known.

Upon arriving "home," however, there is the realization that things aren't quite the same anymore. The ideas and behaviors that previously gave comfort and that seemed to account quite satisfactorily for events in the world are now curiously unsatisfying. So, sooner or later, students gather up the courage to venture forth again to explore new knowledge, skills, or perspectives. Once again, however, they reach a certain point where they experience the terror of newness and they retreat back to more familiar territory. But once more the old familiarities are experienced as inadequate and the process of moving forward begins again. This learning rhythm continues indefinitely as a series of incremental fluctuations.

Finger (1989) has observed this process in the ways people decide to become educators, and he uses the metaphor of home and abroad to describe the process of exploring new interpretive frameworks, skill sets, and bodies of knowledge. It is a telling metaphor for the incremental fluctuations evident when students venture into new intellectual territory. One of the most frequent reactions of someone traveling abroad is to experience an immediate longing for the familiar concurrent with an excitement at the unfamiliar. Much the same dialectical tension between the lure of the unknown and the appeal of the already known is felt during learning.

## Unexpectedness

Students frequently speak of how the most significant episodes in their learning are completely unexpected and take them almost by surprise. In reviewing their learning activities, students will say that they entered a course, workshop, or training program with a clear idea of the specific skills or knowledge they wished to gain. In hindsight, however, they often report that the most important outcome of their educational participation was affective. They speak of the increased feeling of self-confidence they experienced as a result of chang-

ing their views of themselves as teacher-dependent individuals
wholly reliant on external direction to active learners ready to
venture into what were previously seen as intellectual "no-
go" areas. Charnley and Jones (1979) describe this feeling of
self-confidence among literacy students as one of the most
important "enactive" achievements of a national literacy cam-
paign; yet neither teachers nor students often had this goal in
mind as their chief reason for participating in a literacy
program.

When I have conducted critical incident evaluations
with my own students, I am continually surprised by the
results. Students say they experienced transformative break-
throughs in understanding or massive surges in self-confidence from exercises or assignments that to me seem fairly
mundane. Since my students are practicing educators themselves, they often say how they've learned much more by
watching how I ran discussions, gave formal presentations,
tried to involve them in planning what was to happen next,
made concessions on some issues but stayed firm on others,
than they have from any of the content they studied. The
largest single category of responses describes the mix of excitement, liberation, and self-confidence felt as students accomplish something difficult, what I would call experiencing a
sense of agency. But it is the feeling of elation that is etched
in memory, not the specific piece of learning that produced
this.

Research on independent study and self-directed learning has also confirmed the importance of unexpectedness to
students. To most teachers, self-directed learning would seem
to be the least likely learning mode in which to find learners
speaking enthusiastically of the crucial importance of unanticipated aspects of learning. Self-direction seems to imply
the exercise of very close control by learners over the future
course of their learning. Yet learners themselves have stressed
how they take advantage of serendipity in independent study,
of what has been called the "organizing circumstance" (Spear
and Mocker, 1984; Spear, 1988). Learners make full use of
accidental events in their learning. They do not regard taking

advantage of some fortuitious circumstance as an unfortunate straying from the straight and narrow path of self-direction. Unanticipated changes of direction are reported regularly by independent learners and are spoken of as causes for celebration rather than deviant aberrations.

## A Learning Community

It is remarkable how many people use a survival metaphor when speaking of their college experiences. Higher education is frequently seen as a kind of intellectual orientation exercise in which students are dropped off in the middle of unfamiliar intellectual territory and expected to negotiate unknown, difficult terrain before finding the security of base camp. Students recall their entrances into higher education with vivid memories of confusion, fear, and an inability to distinguish between friends or enemies in the anonymous and potentially hostile crowd clustered around them. They speak of their first college experiences with the same sense of stunned alarm expressed by out-of-towners who find themselves in the middle of the New York City subway system for the first time, only to discover that the map of the system is back in the hotel room. In hindsight they might look back on the experience with a feeling of pride that they made it through without irreparable physical or psychological damage, but while they are experiencing it, their only thought is of survival.

When speaking of surviving education, the factor that is recalled as being most crucial is a supportive learning community. Sometimes this community takes the form of a dyadic partnership, sometimes it is a larger group of between four and eight in size. Whatever its size, however, this community functions as a support network of learners who reassure each other that the feelings of inadequacy, confusion, and depression that they experience individually are not idiosyncratic but shared by all.

People will note how important it was to know that when they woke up at 3:00 A.M. panic-stricken about their inability to complete a course, perform a skill, achieve a

---

---

required grade, give a presentation, write a paper, pass a statistics exam, or defend a thesis, that they could call someone. This person, jerked out of sleep (or awake with similar anxieties), would be ready to reassure the anxiety-stricken friend that the experience of panic was one which he or she had also known and survived. The emotional sustenance provided by this kind of peer support is consistently spoken of as being much more important than any information-exchange function the network might have.

## Building on Insights into Learning

The insights regarding how students experience learning described in this chapter obviously have important implications for college teaching. As I pointed out at the beginning of the chapter, however, these insights do not represent the "truth" about learning, nor do they provide the ironclad underpinnings for a theory of teaching. Although they are derived from data culled from thousands of learning reports, these insights are still only indicative of the experiences of an ethnocentric group of students in very specific contexts. So, although they may comprise a "middle range" or "substantive" theory of college learning and teaching (Glaser and Strauss, 1967), they are in no sense an all-inclusive, grand theory. What is most important is that you should make it a regular feature of your practice to try to use the methods and sources reviewed in the previous chapter to try to understand how your own students in your own context experience learning.

# CHAPTER FIVE

# Adjusting Teaching to the Rhythms of Learning

This chapter considers how teachers can make their practice more responsive to the ways students experience learning. I examine each of the insights discussed in the previous chapter to discover its significance for teaching. I do not wish to insist that teaching must always match exactly the rhythms of students, since these rhythms are sometimes disfunctional for them. Many people, if left to themselves, would refuse to explore unfamiliar perspectives, to try out difficult tasks, or to probe the assumptions underlying their habitual ideas and actions. The discomfort and effort involved would be too intimidating. Thus there are times when, as a teacher, you have to ask students to do things that they resist despite your best attempts to explain to them why these are in their own best interests. There are other times when you must be aware of the rhythms, patterns, and experience of learning so that you neither seek to intervene prematurely when this is unnecessary nor stand back when students are becoming comfortable with self-defeating habits.

## Reducing the Impostor Syndrome

Because this syndrome is experienced at such a fundamental psychological level, your efforts alone will probably not be enough to help students shed their perceptions of crippling inadequacy that have been periodically reinforced by feelings of failure experienced over the years. However, you can do some things to reduce the effects the syndrome produces. With care the syndrome can be kept at a level where it is less likely to interfere seriously with the activity of learning.

First, you can regularly affirm a student's sense of self-worth. You can do this by treating respectfully and seriously the most halting and hesitant of contributions made by students in class. You can precede every oral and written criticism or suggestion for improvement you make with a recognition of what is meritorious about a person's work. You can make an effort to refer back to a student's earlier contributions during the later phases of an educational activity.

Second, you can decrease the intensity with which students experience the syndrome by acknowledging how you experience it yourself as a teacher. You should not do this to excess in an orgy of self-flagellation masquerading as modest self-deprecation. But teachers who have credibility in students' eyes can do a great deal to relieve those who suffer from the impostor syndrome by talking about their own occasional feelings of inadequacy as teachers.

Third, you can encourage students to communicate to each other the fact that they feel this way. Knowing that one is not the only person who feels like a fraud and that this perception is, in fact, widespread, is an important factor in reducing its effect. If you have read several learning journals in which the sense of impostorship is revealed, you can ask for permission to read these out to the class. You can inform students of how previous participants experienced, and survived, this syndrome, and you can ask some of these people to return to the current class to talk about this.

### Recognizing Emotionality

The first thing to know about the emotional nature of learning is that it exists. Remember that learning is not a rational, bloodless, ascetic phenomenon. Recall how frequently accounts of significant learning are expressed in terms of feeling—exhilaration, depression, joy, fear, anger, and anxiety. Keep reminding yourself that learning is an activity invested with such significance by students, and one in which their fragile egos face such potentially serious threats, that it would be unnatural for them not to experience it emotionally.

Once we know this as teachers, we are less likely to be thrown by displays of emotion. Instead of regarding them as unseemly disturbances—as offenses against the code of intellectual good manners supposed to pertain in the calmly rational arena of higher education—we come to view them as normal accompaniments to learning. And the pressure to halt displays of emotion as quickly as possible and to return to some mythical state of affective equilibrium becomes less intense. We are more likely to let students' displays of emotion run their natural course and then to analyze, and reflect upon, why they occurred.

It is important to gauge the emotional tenor of your classes. You can do this by asking students directly about their reactions to an activity, although until you've developed the necessary level of trust this will be a rather inhibited, artificial process. You can be as alert as possible to the non-verbal cues of body language, posture, and intonation. You can schedule regular formative evaluation sessions so that students grow accustomed to a discussion of how things are going, of what's working, and what isn't.

When conducting such sessions, you need to pay as much attention to the "negative" emotions such as anger as you do to the more "positive" ones. You can describe your own emotional reactions to what's happening, thereby showing that emotions should not be banned from the classroom. You can send a strong symbolic message that anger will not be punished by asking people to talk about events that have distressed or annoyed them. One useful way to do this is to make use of a critical incident technique in which students are asked to speak about their most intensely experienced "lows" in class. When I have tried this myself, students have often come up to me months after the event to say how symbolically important it was for them to see a teacher inviting and encouraging criticism.

Perhaps the most useful and reliable thing you can do is to ask students to keep personal learning journals as outlined in Chapter Three. Reading these will provide a wealth of material about the emotional life of a class that you could not have predicted in your wildest imaginings. When students are relatively quiescent, it is easy to be deceived into thinking that learning is not being experienced emotionally. This is not the case. It is just that the emotions involved are seen by students as too potentially explosive to be displayed in class. So they are contained in the classroom and then burst out in conversations with intimates, friends, and other learners.

### Fostering Challenge

The insight that students remember as transformative those learning episodes in which some element of challenge was involved has powerful implications for teaching. One of the most laudable characteristics of teachers is their readiness to affirm and encourage learners. Indeed, as my earlier comments on reducing the impostor syndrome indicate, such affirmation is crucial to strengthening a student's sense of self-regard.

Taken to its extreme, however, affirming students can lead to an educational cul-de-sac, in which students feel good about themselves but are never prompted to explore alternative perspectives, to venture into new skill areas, or to scrutinize critically those habitual assumptions underlying their thoughts and actions. To live in a cul-de-sac is quietly comfortable, but it may be self-defeating. But students are sometimes so enclosed within their narrow frames of reference that they are the last to recognize that these may be self-defeating or harmful. Thus often the most important thing you can do for your students is to challenge them with alternative perspectives, new activities, and critical reflection.

## Allowing for Reflective Speculation

One of the most frequent theory-practice discrepancies in college teaching concerns the enthusiasm with which some teachers rush to use small-group approaches in the belief that students will appreciate these since (a) their experience as individuals is being explored to good educational effect and (b) they will prefer participating in small-group work to listening to lectures. In reality, the undoubted value of small-group work is lost almost entirely if you rush into this too early in the belief that students will feel insulted by your obvious authoritarianism if you don't.

In fact, in learning journals and critical incident reports, students often speak of feeling insulted by an overuse of group work or by group work that seems to have little intellectual rationale. This sense of insult comes from the perception that teachers have dumped the responsibility for learning on students, leaving the students awash in ambiguity and confusion. They speak and write of their sense of relief at sometimes being able to occupy the role of attentive listener while an expert who has spent some considerable time exploring an area of intellectual concern lays out its conceptual topography for them. They appreciate the opportunity for reflective speculation afforded by the lecture approach and talk about the experience as one of "luxuriating" in the chance to listen to people speaking in an interesting and informed way about ideas that interest them.

The use of the term *luxuriate* in these accounts is particularly interesting since it encapsulates an erroneous assumption about the nature of learning to which teachers and students both subscribe. Briefly stated, this assumption holds that students must be seen to be learning. In other words, unless students are exhibiting the behaviors associated with actively engaged, participatory learning—such as talking animatedly in small groups or vigorously playing roles in a dramatized simulation—then they are assumed to be experiencing something less than the appropriate level of stimulation one

should expect from college education. It is as if students'
silence is equated with mental inertia.

If this assumption is accepted, then it is easy to see why
teachers and students view silence as something to be avoided
at all costs. How often have you come across a classroom in
which there is total silence? If you did, would not your first
inference be that there was something seriously wrong there?
Yet, if we take the idea of praxis seriously, or if we give any
credence to models of experiential learning, then we must
grant equal importance to periods of reflective speculation
and periods of active engagement. Neither of these is innately
superior to the other. And discussions that are most useful to
students are those distinguished by silence as well as heated
conversation.

In my own teaching I have tried to act on students'
lamentations about the absence of reflective interludes in various ways. I have, as much as possible, begun to err in favor
of depth over breadth where content is concerned. These days
I am much more inclined to ask a student to become thoroughly familiar with one concept, theory, or research procedure than to cover a multiplicity of these. The reading lists
for my courses have decreased markedly, but I require that
what is left is studied very carefully. Instead of asking for
critical comparisons of several theorists, I am likely to require
an in-depth analysis of one.

I have also tried to create more periods for reflection in
my classes. I will announce that I think it's a good idea for
students to spend a few minutes thinking about a new idea or
about what has been said so far, without the pressure of needing to speak to each other or to me. If the quiet is too embarrassing, I might tell people to stretch their legs for ten
minutes while they think. Another idea would be to switch
on a tape recorder and play some unobtrusive, relaxing music
so that people don't become too uncomfortable with the
silence. I do these things with trepidation, since I know that
colleagues and superiors would look askance at my teaching
were they to walk into my classroom at such periods. But
since college classrooms are rarely visited this way unless the

teacher is up for reappointment or tenure, it should be possible to find some way of allowing more reflective interludes in your teaching.

## Adjusting to Incremental Fluctuations

One of the most familiar rhythms of significant learning is that of incremental fluctuation. Learners embrace the unfamiliar while concurrently longing for the familiar. They take two steps forward and one step back. They embark enthusiastically on a conceptual package tour to foreign parts only to find when they get there that the first thing they do is to start calling friends at home.

Being aware of this rhythm means that you are less likely to be discomforted when you see students retreating to older, more habitual ideas and behaviors. If you are unaware of this tendency, the period of retreat might erroneously be interpreted as a sign of regression or slippage and regarded somehow as evidence of your failure. This might lead to the understandable but mistaken temptation to intervene too quickly to force students back on track by pushing them faster than is advisable. Knowing that such temporary retreats by students are natural will relieve you of a great many unnecessary feelings of guilt. You can explain to them that they are experiencing a normal rhythm of learning, and you can prepare them to recognize when this rhythm will occur in the future.

## Building on the Unexpected

If students regard as some of the most significant gains or outcomes of their learning those insights or skills that were not part of the declared educational agenda, then teachers must be wary of sticking to such agendas at all costs. Holding regular formative evaluation and negotiation sessions—occasions when students are asked to review their time with you and to identify significant, valuable aspects of their learning so far—provides you with the opportunity to become aware of these unanticipated, yet valuable aspects of their learning. These sessions will remind you of the need to remain flexible in your teaching, and they will alert you to the error of thinking that changing direction is a sign of amateurism. Such a misconception is sometimes so embedded in teacher education programs that it is hard for teachers to trust their instincts when these suggest that they might depart from preestablished methods, curricula, or objectives.

A very typical scenario in teacher education programs is the following. A primary focal point for assessing new teachers is a practice teaching session. Teaching supervisors visit new teachers in the classrooms over a period of time. The purpose of these visits is to give new teachers systematic feedback on their performance and to gauge whether or not the teacher should be certified or granted the necessary diploma or degree.

Before each visit, the new teacher submits a carefully designed lesson plan, showing the thoughtful integration of what has been learned in the teacher education program into the teacher's own practice. The supervisor sits at the back of the class and checks off the degree of professionalism with which each activity in the lesson plan is performed. Did the lesson begin with the stated introductory exposition lasting the prescribed ten minutes? Was this followed by the planned twenty-minute video? Was the video followed by the anticipated fifteen minutes of focused discussion? Did the teacher get to the planned five-minute wrap-up?

One implicit message in this approach to teacher evaluation is transmitted loud and clear—depart from your script, your lesson plan, at your peril! If a student raises a provocative question in the introductory exposition, the teacher fears to follow it up in any depth in case she is assessed as unfocused, easily diverted, and hence unprofessional. Yet this provocative question may signal an important teachable moment in that the questioner is expressing a concern or interest shared by several others in the group. To refuse to consider such a question because this is not in the script you've written for the class is to deny yourself and your students the vividness and excitement that accompanies a collective focusing on a shared concern. Such teachable moments are frequently unpredicted, but they are often the moments students recall most vividly.

Building on unexpected classroom events is, like most things in teaching, a question of balance. You can't treat every unanticipated eventuality in class as a profound teachable moment. If you keep changing what you intended to do in a way that appears capricious to students, then your credibility will be undermined. Teachers who have no clear organizing vision and who seem to be borne aloft on whatever intellectual winds are blowing that day in class, risk being perceived as flighty and insubstantial, of having nothing to offer.

When you do make last-minute changes in what you had declared you would be doing, the reasons for these changes need to be explained to students. This is partly a matter of common courtesy and respect. More important, though, if you have a habit of saying you'll do one thing and then doing another—without explaining carefully the rationale for your change of mind—then you reduce the chance that students will ever trust you. So, leave yourself open to the possibility of change and follow your instincts even when these diverge from your plan, but make sure that you take students with you by informing them fully about the reasons behind the changes.

### Fostering a Learning Community

The survival metaphor often invoked by students in describing their progress through higher education focuses on the importance of learning communities. Knowing the importance of such emotionally sustaining support networks should alert you to the need to seize on opportunities to assist their development when these arise. You can encourage peer teaching (Whitman, 1988) or "parrainage" (Goldschmid, 1988) among students. You can urge the formation of learning partnerships (Robinson, Saberton, and Griffin, 1985). You can publish students' addresses and phone numbers early on in a class and suggest that people form car pools to get to and from class. You can ask students to write on poster paper what they feel are their most important skills, what they most want to learn, and what dreams they have for the future and then display these publicly so each student gets a sense of the interests and enthusiasms of others in the group.

Some informal clustering will always occur and you want to avoid forcing it at an unnaturally fast pace, but most teachers could probably pay considerably more attention to it than they do. In the doctoral program at Teachers College, Columbia University, in which I teach—the AEGIS program (Adult Education through Guided Independent Study)—students are encouraged to form collaborative dissertation groups. Members of these groups work together on formulating dissertation proposals, drafting and field-testing instruments, conducting literature reviews, and sometimes even analyzing each other's data.

We have also abolished letter grades completely, moving to a pass/fail system. One reason for doing this is to reduce competition. In classes where students know that on a bell curve only a few A's are available, they will be reluctant to share insights and information with each other. They will avoid letting their guard down to reveal their real feelings. They will refuse to share references, sources, or original ideas with each other for fear of losing valuable ground in the quest for one of those prized high grades. A common reaction will be to ask, "Why should I let someone else get the benefit from all my effort and cheat me out of my reward?" So competitive grading is directly antithetical to the creation of a supportive, emotionally sustaining learning network.

It has been astonishing to see how working in collaborative dissertation groups has affected students. Long after their graduation, students recall the most significant aspect of their doctoral program being the interpersonal learning and the development of a collaborative sensitivity among group members. Learning how to acknowledge differences, avoid "groupthink," create group codes, set limits, and administer fair sanctions to lazy members are spoken of as more memorable than either the formal focus of the dissertation study or the content of the course work in the program. Students say that the intensity of the small-group experience will stay with them long after they have finished their doctoral study. Interestingly, this is as true for students in groups that are marked by strong personality clashes as it is for those in groups that appear well integrated.

## Taking Account of Learning Styles

On the face of it, a simple proposition seems to hold the key to responsive teaching: If teachers wish to connect with as many students as possible, all they need to do is to find out about the learning styles these students exhibit and then adjust their teaching exercises and materials to the spread of styles revealed. For several reasons the appealing simplicity of this idea does not match the complex fluidity of learning.

There is, first of all, considerable confusion among teachers and researchers about what exactly comprises a learning style (Kolb, 1981; Perry, 1988). In particular, cognitive style (the internal mediatory processes by which we interpret new experiences and sensory stimuli) is often mistakenly equated with preferred learning style (the habitual ways we conduct learning activities, such as setting goals, identifying resources, or generating evaluative criteria). There is also confusion about how, and whether, preferred learning styles reflect or relate to developmental stages in young adulthood and maturity (Claxton and Murrell, 1987).

Some researchers have raised doubts about whether the belief in a consistent learning style across a lifetime has much empirical validity. For example, Kolb (1983) has documented research showing that people's styles change over time. I have scored very differently on the same learning style inventories completed at different times in my life. According to the nature of the learning task and learning domain involved, I can appear linear or lateral, field-dependent or field-independent, divergent or convergent. Even research conducted on students who, superficially, appear to be exemplars of field independence (self-taught experts) shows how these same people exhibit strong elements of field dependence when they describe their preferred learning orientations.

It is also true that in determining how someone is going to learn something a number of variables other than an individual's preferred learning style are of equal or greater importance. Chief among these are the nature of the learning task, the student's level of learning readiness, the student's previous experience and knowledge in this area, the student's and the teacher's personalities, the personalities of other learners, the political ethos of the educational institution, and the dominant values and traditions of the culture of which the student is a member. So the idea of teaching to easily identifiable learning styles, while superficially simple, is in reality highly complex.

In fact, rather than teachers always adjusting their practice to account for students' preferred learning styles, a good educational case can be made for doing precisely the opposite. In other words, instead of affirming the habitual, comfortable ways your students go about their learning—some of which may involve deeply etched, self-defeating habits—you should think about introducing them to alternative modes of learning.

If you provide field-independent learners (those who like to work in isolation as they set their own goals and conduct their own learning efforts) with a steady diet of independent study activities you are certainly likely to make these learners feel comfortable and to confirm in them the style they naturally prefer. The problem is that when such people are confronted with the real life need to work collaboratively—in team projects at a workplace or in a political movement—they are totally thrown by the experience. It has always struck me as ironic that so much research conducted by college students is done in isolation. If students collaborate on a paper, a master's thesis, or a doctoral dissertation, all manner of problems concerning plagiarism are raised. Yet, as soon as people need to research something outside of educational settings, they are almost always required to work in collaborative teams. So the learning orientations encouraged within the academy are sometimes the most disfunctional that could be imagined in terms of helping students prepare for learning outside.

This is why the development of self-direction in students falls short of being a satisfactory organizing vision for college teaching. In real life most of us intersperse self-direction with cooperation. We alternate valuing independence with the need to work interdependently. We need collective involvement as well as individual enterprise. In terms of changing individual destinies, it is often collective efforts that make all the difference. So many changes in people's individual lives are linked to broader social and political movements that being able to contribute to these movements, and to work interdependently within them, is crucial for personal survival.

For all these reasons, and because most learning episodes exhibit contextual variables and demands that require a variety of learning responses, it is sometimes important to teach *against* students' preferred learning styles. If you have the students' best interests at heart, you may well decide that the last thing they need is to be confirmed in a comfortable, but very narrowly focused, learning style. Far better to introduce them to a diversity of ways of planning and conducting learning.

The principle of diversity should be engraved on every teacher's heart. In evaluating a teacher's performance, or in judging the merit of an educational approach, one of the first things I look for is diversity. Are teachers using a range of teaching approaches? Do they use visual materials as well as relying on oral and written communication? Do they alternate opportunities for independent study with group collaboration? Do they mix lectures, discussions role plays, and simulations? Do they allow for periods of reflective analysis?

Keeping diversity at the forefront serves two important functions. On the one hand, you stand a good chance of connecting to the preferred learning style of most of your students at some point in your teaching. At this point, they will feel comfortable with, and affirmed in, their learning. On the other hand, you will probably introduce most students in your classes to learning modes and orientations that are new to them. Their repertoire of learning styles will thus be enlarged, and they will be more likely to flourish in a greater range of settings outside the academy than would otherwise have been the case.

# CHAPTER SIX

# Lecturing Creatively

Of all the methods of college teaching, the lecture is probably the most frequently abused (Brown, 1980, 1987). Many teachers are socialized into believing that lecturing is the normal way to teach and that it should only be abandoned when unusual circumstances demand this. It is surprising how many professors in programs of teacher education, whose practice presumably exhibits an insightful understanding of teaching, rely on lectures as the chief means of encouraging learning. Even at professional conferences of teachers—the places where one might expect a strong reliance on participatory learning approaches—session after session features a lecture format. At such conferences I have sat through numerous one-hour presentations where presenters devoted fifty-five minutes to an uninterrupted, rambling examination of apparently irrelevant minutiae delivered in a sleep-inducing monotone. After the session moderator has finally forced the speaker to stop talking, five minutes of frantic questions ensue. Many lecturers seem to assume their inalienable right to bore.

Because of such abuses and because of the authoritarian, teacher-centered nature of lecturing, the method has often been pronounced dead. Yet, for having expired so frequently, its corpse displays a remarkable liveliness. Indeed, those who are prone to read the last rites at one time in their thinking often find that they are resuscitating the corpse at a later point.

For example, over two decades ago Freire (1970) associated lecturing with the worst kind of banking education, that is, with the approach whereby experts see themselves as depositing knowledge in the empty vaults of students' minds. Recently, however, he says that "we have to recognize that not all kinds of lecturing is banking education. You can still be very critical lecturing. . . . The question is not banking lectures or no lectures, because traditional teachers will make reality opaque whether they lecture or lead discussions. A liberating teacher will illuminate reality even if he or she lectures. The question is the content and dynamism of the lecture, the approach to the object to be known. Does it critically re-orient students to society? Does it animate their critical thinking or not?" (Shor and Freire, 1987, p. 40).

As Freire recognizes, we should be wary of dismissing lectures completely just because they have been delivered so frequently in an authoritarian or mind-numbing manner. A misused method calls into question the expertise of those misusing it, not the validity of the method itself. We have to acknowledge that in college settings both students and teachers have such strong expectations that lecturing will be a major educational method that its continuing prominence is something of a foregone conclusion. The challenge we face as teachers is to make our lectures as enlivening and critically stimulating as possible. It is to meeting this challenge that the guidelines and techniques suggested in the following paragraphs are devoted.

## Be Clear About Why You Choose to Lecture

As is the case with any educational method, you need to be quite clear why you are choosing to lecture at any particular time (McKeachie, 1986). Avoid falling into the routine of lecturing just because this is what is expected. Make sure that your decision is based on very clear reasons why you think this is appropriate. Some of the most common reasons for lecturing follow:

*To establish the broad outlines of a body of material:* In a lecture you can paint in broad intellectual sweeps. If you want to present students with contrasting schools of thought, or if you want to group a confusing variety of opinions into general interpretive categories, then a lecture is a good means of conveying this breadth of ideas.

*To set guidelines for independent study:* In lectures you can set the stage for more intensive follow-up study through discussion and individual reading. Rather than having students plunge into a highly detailed body of content, with the risk that they'll be unable to focus on what is important and relevant, you can highlight the key questions their study should be seeking to answer.

*To model intellectual attitudes you hope to encourage in students:* A lecture can be a convenient medium for displaying the standards of intellectual rigor and critical analysis you seek to encourage. If you want students to be critical of their own ideas, to be ready to support their arguments with evidence, and to be able to explore alternative perspectives and interpretations, then you must be ready to model these attitudes and actions in your lectures. Also, by publicly grappling with the complexities of an idea, you can demonstrate that learning is a process in which experiencing difficulties is not a sign of failure or a source of shame.

*To encourage learners' interest in a topic:* A lecture can be an enlivening, inspirational event that nurtures in students an enthusiasm for a previously unexplored topic. This can happen when students are infected by your personal animation and passion or when you establish for them direct and important connections between the topic reviewed and their own concerns.

*To set the moral culture for discussions:* You can increase enormously the chances of subsequent discussions being focused, rigorous, and respectful if your preliminary lectures set the right tone. If you respectfully explore viewpoints that oppose your own, if you are ready to acknowledge facts and interpretations that are "inconvenient" because they undermine your position, and if you refuse to wrap up your comments with a neatly formulated, final conclusion, then you send a strong message that these are the behaviors you expect of discussion participants.

## Research Your Audience

It is a major mistake to deliver a lecture as if the audience were irrelevant. If you don't know or care who is listening to you, then you may as well record your comments at home before a video camera and send the tape to whomever requests it. If at all possible you should find out beforehand something about the culture and concerns of your audience. Doing this will bring you several benefits. You will be more likely to use language that is accessible to your audience, not exclusionary. You will be able to demonstrate connections between your topic and your listeners' concerns in terms students understand and are convinced by. You will be able to focus on the common experiences, problems, and dilemmas of your audience and so keep their interest. You will run less risk of making needlessly offensive remarks, jokes in poor taste, or incomprehensible allusions.

If you cannot find out about your audience beforehand, take some time at the beginning of the lecture to do preliminary research. Suggest some themes that you might consider in that day's session and ask for a show of hands indicating which are of the most interest. Ask for suggestions for possible themes from the floor, and as these are made turn them back to the audience by asking for a vote on whether any of them concern a large enough portion of the audience to make it worth your while addressing them.

When I speak to an audience of teachers outside my institution, I often preface my talk by mentioning a number of common professional roles (instruction, counseling, curriculum design, and so on) and asking for a show of hands on how many of the audience see themselves performing each of these roles. I then invite those who have not been covered by one of the roles mentioned to shout out how they see their chief pedagogic responsibilities. I also give a number of possible settings in which educators work (colleges, schools, the media, health education, corporate training, libraries, community action projects, and so on) and ask my audience by a show of hands to tell me where most of them work.

Again, those whose work settings have not been covered are invited to shout these out. The information I get from the answers to these brief questions at least gives me a sense of whom I'm talking to and what some of their concerns might be.

If there is time, I might put people into groups of three or four and ask them to spend ten minutes or so talking about the most problematic dilemmas they face in their work. At the end of this time, each of these small groups then chooses one of these dilemmas to suggest as a possible topic for me to address in my lecture. As groups shout out their different choices, several clusters usually emerge, and I then try to make sure that I give plenty of time to discussing these during my presentation. Of course, this can be embarrassing when the dilemmas they suggest are ones to which I have given no forethought. If this happens, then I will admit that these are dilemmas I have not been asked to examine before and that my remarks on them will, therefore, be tentative. I also assure them that before I make a presentation to a similar group in the future I will give some thought to these unfamiliar (to me, at any rate) dilemmas and make sure that I have something to say about them when they are next raised.

## Pace Your Presentation

The average attention span for listening to an uninterrupted lecture has been estimated at somewhere between twelve and twenty minutes (Bligh, 1972; Brown, 1980; Rogers, 1989), and it is a good idea to pace your presentation with this in mind. Since many lectures are planned for periods of sixty to ninety minutes, there is obviously a serious discrepancy between what research tells us people can absorb and what curriculum organizers believe they can tolerate. Being aware of this discrepancy, I am sometimes tempted to show up and speak for the first twenty minutes of the alloted time and then refuse to say anything else until the audience has divided into small groups to discuss the relevance of my opening remarks for another ten minutes. Alternatively, I am tempted to insist that the lecture be a question-and-answer session with its central themes determined by the audience's interests.

These approaches can sometimes work wonderfully well, and listeners can experience a real release as they take control of the content and format of the session. But I have also experienced this strategy backfiring in a very embarrassing way when my refusal to speak for more than twenty minutes, or to give an opening statement at all, has left an audience feeling puzzled, anxious, and angry. As Chapter Five showed, many people enjoy the chance to luxuriate in listening to a lecture. My insistence that I am denying them this pleasure for their own good can result in little more than a sense of irritated confusion settling upon the entire gathering.

If you find yourself in a position where you are regularly expected to give lectures, there is probably little chance of reversing the expectation that your voice will dominate the occasion. There are, however, many ways you can take account of the twenty-minute attention span and pace your presentation accordingly. You can begin by asking the kinds of brief, information-gathering questions already described in the previous section. You can open up with a brief critical incident exercise. You can announce at the outset that you will break up your material into twenty- or thirty-minute chunks of exposition, but that after each chunk you will invite ten minutes of questioning. Before each portion of a lecture, you can begin with a new critical incident question to focus students' minds on the themes you will address in the upcoming chunk. You can allow a stretch break of a couple of minutes three or four times during a ninety-minute session.

You can also stop after twenty or thirty minutes of your exposition to say to an audience something like the following: "Well, I've talked about a lot of complex issues and concepts so far, and I suspect that many of you are feeling confused right now. So why not spend five minutes silently reviewing the notes you've made so far, and then spend five minutes discussing with the person sitting next to you what you think is (a) the most important point made up to now and (b) the most confusing idea expressed so far. Or, if you don't want to be forced into conversation, then just spend the whole ten minutes thinking about what I've said up to now. Then we'll spend ten minutes dealing with any questions or comments you might have." Using these techniques to pace your presentation means that a ninety-minute lecture might end up with the following sequence:

### Example of a Paced Presentation

*1–10 minutes:* Research the audience. (Ask questions about listeners' backgrounds, current work contexts, and common concerns, and ask for votes on possible themes you might address.)

*10–20 minutes:* Critical incident. (Ask audience members to think back over the past six months and write down brief details about an episode of significance in their experience that connects to the theme of the presentation. Then invite any audience members who wish to do so to read out what they've written.)

*20–40 minutes:* First formal presentation.

*40–50 minutes:* Question period on issues raised by the first formal presentation.

*50–55 minutes:* Stretch break.

*55–75 minutes:* Second formal presentation.

*75–85 minutes:* Question period on issues raised by the second formal presentation.

*85–90 minutes:* Final statement on themes covered in the two formal presentations and in the question interludes.

As you can see, of the ninety minutes alloted to the lecture, only forty-five are actually taken up by the presenter's voice— the two twenty-minute formal presentations and the final five-minute summary.

## Personalize Your Presentation

Too many lecturers make the mistake of going straight to a level of conceptual abstraction with which they are comfortable but which leaves audience members feeling dazed and intimidated. So be aware of this and try to think of ways of personalizing your topic. Draw on examples from your own life that illustrate the general processes you are examining. Use anecdotes from current events, films, sports, or prime-time television programs that connect to your themes. Whenever possible, represent complex intellectual ideas or connections between concepts by using analogies and metaphors that are familiar to people.

For example, when I give a lecture on critical thinking, I avoid speaking only in general terms about the processes of reflective skepticism, contextual awareness, imaginative speculation, and assumption analysis that I see as being at the core of this concept. I give examples from my own life of how I have experienced each of these processes in my teaching, my intimate relationships, my political involvements, or my parenting. I talk about how these processes can be seen to work themselves out in the actions of characters in films, television dramas, or popular novels. If I'm discussing teaching methods, I give examples from my own practice of times when these have worked and when they have backfired, and I try to describe graphically and honestly how this felt.

Personalizing lectures in these ways serves three important functions. First, it helps provide familiar, accessible points of entry to complex ideas. Second, it captures an audience's attention to see a remote figure speaking in a personally revealing way. Third, your readiness to talk publicly about aspects of your life outside your role as an educator helps to create the sense of authenticity discussed in Chapter Twelve. Students warm to descriptions of abstract intellectual processes that spring from personal experience. So, unlike some teachers who maintain that personalizing a topic muddies the clear water of intellectual analysis with emotional sludge, I believe that students connect strongly to personalized descriptions.

## Speak from Notes

As a general rule, lectures read from prewritten scripts come across as dull and predictable. Since the lecturer knows what is coming next, it is hard to maintain the element of surprise. So, unless you are possessed of an unusual degree of dramatic flair, or unless you have the time to rehearse your delivery in a way that introduces a dynamic range of pitch, gesture, and emphasis, I would not advise reading your lecture. This is not a hard and fast rule, and if the terror induced by the prospect of speaking without every word having being previously written down is so overwhelming that you freeze up or are reduced to babbling incoherence, then you should obviously have the safety net of the full text of your presentation in front of you. But if you reflect on your own experience as a listener, you will be convinced of the appeal of a presentation that appears spontaneous and that uses idiomatic language.

Speaking from notes is definitely not the same as unplanned, extemporaneous talking. Skeleton notes are carefully drawn up and depict an ordered and systematic progression of ideas, but they have the advantage of allowing the speaker the freedom to digress and to include personal anecdotes when these seem appropriate. If you are speaking from a prepared text, it is difficult to respond to questions from the floor that do not conform to the order in which your ideas unfold themselves in this text. If, however, you have one or two pages of skeleton notes, then your eye can quickly fall on the section relevant to the question asked and you can respond more quickly and confidently.

An example of skeleton lecture notes will probably make this clearer. Exhibit 1 reprints some notes I have used for a presentation on understanding critical thinking.

Speaking from notes is premised on the assumption that you have a thorough knowledge of your topic so that a word or phrase will trigger all kinds of ideas and associations. In an ideal world, no one would be giving a lecture on a topic with which they did not feel thoroughly familiar. But we do not live in an ideal world, and sometimes you may find yourself forced to lecture on a subject with which you have only a fairly superficial familiarity. In this case it is probably better to rely on a more detailed outline, perhaps even to read a speech, though this should be kept as short as possible.

I would also suggest that you make a point of distributing copies of your lecture notes to audience members after your presentation. If you announce at the beginning of a lecture that students will receive copies of the notes you are working from at the end of the session, then they are freed from the laborious task of trying to write down every word you say. They can concentrate on the flow of your argument, jotting down notes on things that occur to them while you are speaking, but avoiding getting writer's cramp from trying to produce what is essentially a verbatim transcript of your remarks. They have a chance to sift through your comments, making note only of things that have some special meaning for them.

It's a mistake to distribute copies of your notes at the beginning of your lecture, since many people will spend the first ten or fifteen minutes reading these notes rather than listening to what you're saying. It is asking too much of most people not to do this, so it is best to remove this temptation from them, but to reassure them with a promise that copies of your lecture notes will be distributed to them at the end of your presentation.

### Use Visual Aids

Wherever possible, try to use graphic depictions of some of your main points and try to demonstrate connections between

## Exhibit 1. Skeleton Lecture Notes.

*Understanding Critical Thinking*

*Introduction:* Conceptual confusion—diverse traditions

- Frankfurt School
- Psychoanalysis
- Analytic Philosophy

*Definition:* Three-stage process

1. Becoming aware we have assumptions
2. Identifying assumptions
3. Scrutinizing their accuracy and validity

*Four Key Questions*

1. Why is it important?
   - Central to concept of adulthood
   - Central to democratic process
   - Liberates us from constraints of present
2. Can it be taught? Yes! But:
   - Needs praxis of action and reflection
   - Takes time: lifelong process
   - Based on trust between learners and teachers
   - Developed in specific contexts
3. Are educators the people to teach it?
   Sometimes! Also friends, colleagues, therapists, political leaders
   (N.B., Teachers are also learners in critical thinking episodes.)
4. Should it be taught? Yes! But it involves *RISK.*
   To teachers:
   - Anger and resentment of anxiety-stricken learners
   - Gaining "subversive," "difficult" reputation
   To learners:
   - Threat of unfamiliar—loss of past rationalizations
   - "Betrayal" of intimates—cultural suicide

*Major Components of Critical Thinking*

Assumption analysis—identifying commonsense assumptions
Contextual awareness—recognizing culturally created nature of ideas
Imaginative speculation—exploring alternatives to habitual ideas
Reflective skepticism—mistrust of　—final solutions
　　　　　　　　　　　　　　　　　　—monocausal explanations
　　　　　　　　　　　　　　　　　　—divinely ordained truths

*Processes of Critical Thinking—Typical Stages*

- Trigger:　• Discrepancy/anomaly/contradiction—what is/should be
　　　　　　• Disorienting trauma (unemployment, bereavement, divorce)
　　　　　　• "Peak" experience of "coming home"

**Exhibit 1. Skeleton Lecture Notes, Cont'd**

- Fluctuation between denial and acceptance of anomaly, trauma
- Search for others in same situation—mutual exploration
- Reframing assumptions to fit reality
- Integration into action
  (N.B., A never ending process—continuous spiral)

*How Critical Thinking Is Experienced*
1. Incremental fluctuation—2 steps forward, 1 step back: home and abroad
2. Multifaceted—threatening as well as liberating
3. Context-specific—can be critical in one domain and uncritical in another (examples—marriage, politics, workplace)
4. Process not outcome—never achieve state of complete critical awareness
5. Grieving process—mourning for lost assumption/golden era of certainty

*Final Questions*
1. Ethical dimensions—Are we always justified in encouraging critical thinking in learners who resist this?
2. How far is critical thinking itself a cultural construct? How far is my interpretation a reflection of my own biography and culture?
3. Risks—Are these worth the benefits? (exclusion, cultural suicide, psychological turbulence, political oppression, "bad" reputation)
4. Freeze—Does critical thinking lead to a relativistic freeze, a refusal to make commitments?
5. Assumptions—To what extent are my own ideas based on untested assumptions?

these in some visually appealing way. This provides another channel through which students can interpret your ideas, and it will be especially appealing to those who think visually. If you lack graphic talent, you can usually find someone who can translate your ideas into visual representations. Even listing your main points on an overhead helps learners to follow the progression of your argument. Again, you should announce at the outset that you will be distributing copies of any visual aids you use at the end of the lecture. Alternatively, you can distribute copies of the handout at appropriate points in your talk, thereby preventing people from having to strain their necks and eyes to see what you've put on the screen.

Over the years I have tried to put some of the ideas I discuss in my lectures into visual form. As someone who does not think visually I have had to borrow other people's graphics or have people who are visually inclined take my ideas and convert these. Figure 1 is a graphic I have often used. Drawn from a book by Larry Daloz (1986) on teaching and mentoring, it depicts the delicate balance teachers need to strike between supporting and challenging students.

Another graphic I have used (Figure 2) was prepared for me by a designer who had read my book *Understanding and Facilitating Adult Learning* (1986) and who tried to portray visually some of its central themes and the relationships between them.

## Use Critical Incidents

Critical incidents can be used at two points in a lecture: before the formal presentation begins as a way of attracting students' attention and helping you gain a sense of their predominant concerns and in the intervals between twenty- to thirty-minute chunks of your lecture to help students focus on the themes to be covered in the forthcoming portion. Let me say something about why, and how, I believe critical incidents should be used in these ways.

**Figure 1. Balancing Challenge and Support
and the Effects of This on Learners.**

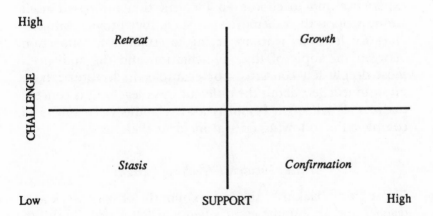

*Source:* Daloz, 1986. Used by permission.

Figure 2. Understanding and Facilitating Adult Learning:
A Theory in Use.

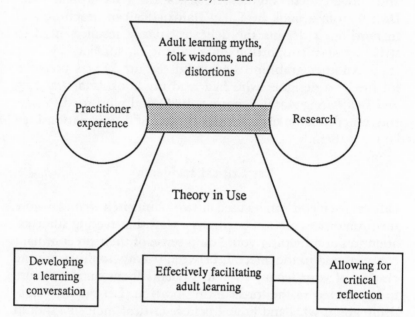

Critical incidents are brief written (or spoken) depictions of vividly remembered events. In a critical incident exercise, people are asked to review some category of their experience and to choose an incident that impressed itself strongly upon their memories. As such, they provide valuable clues for lecturers who are trying to establish a connection between the topic of their presentation and the audience's most deeply felt concerns. For example, in lectures I have given to teachers about the different ways teaching is conceptualized, I will often begin by asking audience members to complete the following critical incident exercise:

### Critical Incident: Teaching "Highs"

Please think back over the last six months of your work as a teacher and choose the event when you felt a real "high" of excitement and fulfillment—a time when you said to yourself,

"This is what teaching is all about; this is what makes it all worthwhile." Write down a brief description of this event, making special note of where and when it occurred, who was involved, and what made the event so enjoyable.

After ten minutes or so, I call for the audience's attention and ask people to volunteer to read out whatever they have written. As they read out their responses, I offer my interpretation of what the event signifies by saying something like "That sounds as if you really value students' opinions" or "That sounds as if you think that debate and disagreement are healthy aspects of discussions." I give those who have read out their responses the chance to agree, disagree, or voice an alternative interpretation. After listening to four or five of these responses from the audience, I proceed with my lecture.

Usually, several of the themes covered in my remarks connect to some of these critical incident responses, and I am able to mention these as I go along. Even if there are no connections between my remarks and these responses, this is useful in itself since I can remark on this contrast and on how interesting it is that published research or my own thinking can so diverge from teachers' real concerns.

One final point on this technique. Critical incidents generally work best if audience members have some familiarity with the topic to be discussed, some views about it, and some relevant experience they can review. If the audience has no knowledge or experience of the topic to be covered it is probably best to avoid the technique.

## Leave with a Question

The most frequently quoted axiom about good lecturing is "Tell them what you're going to say, say it, then tell them what you've said." This advice has always struck me as somewhat pedestrian and more than a little patronizing. Although it is important to explain the purpose of your presentation and then to discuss what you said you would discuss, I think it is a mistake to finish by "telling them what you've said."

The repetition in this approach can be annoying and insulting to students since it implies that they are too dense to understand the point of a lecture the first or second time around so you are hammering it into them a third and final time. But more important, "Telling them what you've said" establishes a sense of definitive closure that inhibits further intellectual inquiry.

In contradiction to this axiom, I always try to end my lectures with questions about the truth of what I have just been asserting. I refer to criticisms of some of my points. I acknowledge the unproven assumptions and untested beliefs upon which some of my ideas are based. I try to identify the most contentious, unresolved issues in my lecture and encourage students to investigate these. This tends to surprise students (always a good idea where keeping an audience awake is concerned), and it creates a future-oriented, inquiring state of mind. The audience's last memory of your lecture is of the questions you urged them to explore further.

## See Yourself as Your Audience Sees You

Finally, one of the best ways of improving your lecturing is to find some way of standing outside your practice so that you can hear and see yourself as closely as possible to the way in which your audience hears and sees you. There are several ways you can do this. You should encourage students to tell you about aspects of your lecturing style that both help and hinder their learning. This can be done by talking informally with them, by reading any learning journals they submit to you, or by administering some kind of evaluative checklist at the end of your lectures.

Perhaps the best thing you can do is to arrange to have some of your lectures videotaped so that you can watch your own performance. This can sometimes be very embarrassing, but it is never less than instructive. It is probably the only way you can catch your verbal and visual tics, the annoying habits of which you may be totally unaware, but which interfere with the audience's comprehension of your presentation.

If videotaping is not technically possible, you can make an audio tape of your lectures and listen for ways to improve your pacing, pitch, and delivery.

You can also ask a colleague whose opinion you trust, and with whom you have no feeling that you might lose face if your flaws are revealed, to observe you lecturing. Ask this person to pay particular attention to the features of your lecturing style that distract attention from the content of your comments. To protect your self-esteem, you should also ask for an indication of those features that are visually arresting, inspirational, and helpful to students' understanding. Whatever way you find to do this, seeing yourself through the eyes of your audience is absolutely essential if you want to be clear, critically stimulating, and responsive in your lecturing.

※ CHAPTER SEVEN

# Preparing for Discussion

Ask any group of college teachers which method they feel is most appropriate to a higher educational environment and the chances are that a large number of them, possibly a majority, will choose discussion. As a teaching method, discussion seems democratic and participatory. Those who proclaim its benefits do so because it appears to place teachers and students on an equal footing, because it implies that everyone has some useful contribution to make to the educational effort, and because it claims to be successful in actively involving students in the educational process (Brookfield, 1985a, 1990d).

What is sometimes forgotten, however, is that discussion groups have a powerful psychodynamic dimension to them. They can easily become competitive emotional battlegrounds with participants vying for recognition and affirmation from each other and from the discussion leader. American culture places great emphasis on the confident extrovert, and the glib, articulate group member is often regarded as more of an educational success than his or her quietly reflective colleague. Sometimes the frequency of a student's verbal contributions—almost regardless of their lucidity or relevance—becomes the criterion for judging participation.

Patterns of participation tend to be created, and fixed, early in a group's life. By the third meeting of a discussion-based course, discrepancies in communication between gar-

rulous and silent members are usually well established. This
pecking order of communication is self-fulfilling; the longer
a student remains silent, the more intimidating is the prospect
of eventual participation. I know this from personal experience. With my personal mixture of arrogance and introver-
sion I never wanted to contribute to discussions in my student
days unless what I was going to say would be universally
admired. I would spend minutes silently rehearsing my contribution to make it penetrating and profound, only to find
that when I thought it was sufficiently brilliant the discussion
had moved on and my rehearsed comment was no longer
relevant. The longer I had to wait to make my first contribution (I had a personal rule that I would always say something—anything—during the first meeting, just to be noticed)
the more nervous and apprehensive I became. So that when
the glorious moment arrived and I spoke my piece, what came
out was generally garbled.

Because students invest discussions with considerable
emotional significance, their need to perform well (that is, to
talk frequently and confidently) becomes inextricably bound
up with their self-esteem. In such an emotionally charged
atmosphere it is easy to interpret comments critical of one's
own opinions as personal attacks. When disagreement is
equated with aggression, reflective thought becomes impossible. This is why it is so important for teachers to model in
their lectures and discussions a readiness to invite critical
scrutiny of their most deeply held ideas.

Despite the psychodynamic complexity of discussion, a
great many claims, some of them somewhat portentous, have
been made for this method. American educators, particularly
educators of adults, have seen a role for discussion that
extends far beyond the classroom. After World War II, discussion was regarded by some as the most important educational
contribution that could be made to the reconstruction effort.
Lindeman (1945) claimed the neighborhood discussion group
was essential to the maintenance of democracy and, hence, to
world peace. If citizens participated in discussion groups,
they would learn democratic habits, be able to see through

the inflated claims of demagogues, and develop critical anten-
nae about the tendency of politicians to foist propaganda on
them. Essert (1948) advised Americans to regard participation
in discussion groups as a substitute for the experience of community that had been denied to so many as industrialism
advanced, as extended families declined, and as geographical
and occupational mobility increased.

These claims have been tempered in more recent
times, but there is no doubt that in certain disciplines
within the humanities and the social sciences discussion is
regarded as the quintessential college educational process.
Sometimes the aura surrounding this process becomes
almost mystical; in an earlier work of mine, for example, I
wrote that "to participate in discussion—in the collaborative externalization, exploration, and critical analysis of personally significant meaning systems—is to realize one's
adulthood to its fullest extent" (Brookfield, 1986, p. 140).
But despite the mystical tone that sometimes creeps into
writing about discussion and despite the fact that flexibility
and risk taking are elements central to the process, it is a
mistake to see discussions as wholly unplanned, spontaneous events. Good discussions do not just happen. By taking
several preparatory steps, you can greatly increase the
chances that something meaningful will occur.

### Avoid Guided Discussions

In advocating that teachers prepare carefully for discussion, I
might sound as though I am suggesting that discussions be
guided toward some previously defined end point. This is the
opposite of what I believe discussion is all about. You should
certainly be clear about why you are using discussion methods, and you should be aware of some of the effects it can
have on students, but you must never go into the learning
conversation with the outcomes of your efforts clearly defined
beforehand. This is fine for other educational methods, but
not for discussion. If you enter a supposedly free-ranging discussion in which you are asking students to create meaning

through a process of collaborative inquiry, it is basically dishonest to have established privately what these meanings are to be. As soon as students realize the discussion is moving towards the point you have in mind, their interest will flag. And the discussion will become an exercise in manipulation, not an example of participation in authentic discourse.

Teachers sometimes use discussions for three particular reasons: problem solving, concept exploration, and attitude change. In problem solving the purpose is to explore the nature of a problem and then investigate alternative solutions. Discussions aimed at concept exploration seek to revise concepts that have been introduced in lectures or assigned readings. Discussions designed to change attitudes try to engender in learners what teachers define as desirable attitudes. These three kinds of discussions are sometimes called "guided," "controlled," and "directed" or "teaching" discussions.

"Guiding" a discussion, however, is a contradiction in terms. Since discussion is, by definition, a free and open process an end point cannot be specified in advance. Yet, in problem-solving discussions the problems to be solved are usually selected in advance by leaders, as is the range of alternative solutions to be explored. Rarely do groups engage in problem posing (Freire, 1970) or problem setting (Schön, 1983), that is, in collaboratively identifying problematic aspects of reality such as major discrepancies between ideals and actuality, between rhetoric and action.

In concept-exploration discussions the cognitive outcomes of the activity are often set in the teacher's mind. Watkins (1975, p. 7) describes how "the tutor's sense of responsibility for the group—his determination that the ground should be covered—can deter individual students from clarifying their own experience of the material under discussion. In other words, the learning which takes place is sanctioned by the tutor and not necessarily what the student most needs." In attitude-change discussions, the whole purpose of the activity is to help students assimilate attitudes defined by leaders in advance.

The manipulation endemic to these discussions will soon

enough be perceived by students. Depending on the context
and the power relationships in play, students will either challenge the leader or try to feed back to the leader what students
perceive to be the correct attitudes and opinions. Alternatively,
they may just decide to opt out of such a dishonest exercise in
manipulation by leaving the group or by mentally distancing
themselves from everything that's happening.

Paterson (1970, p. 47) describes guided discussions as
"counterfeit" discussions.

> One inevitably wonders how many . . . counter-
> feit discussions are staged in adult classes by
> tutors whose confidence in their own preferred
> views disables them from taking the views of
> their students with the utmost seriousness
> required of all the participants in authentic edu-
> cational dialogue. I am referring less to the asser-
> tive and dogmatic tutor than to the kind of tutor
> who unobtrusively and skillfully synthesizes the
> various discussion contributions of his students,
> by judicious selection and emphasis, into a neatly
> structured and rounded proposition or body of
> propositions, which are then presented as the
> "conclusions" of the "class discussion" although
> they have in fact been evolved by the tutor, who
> has ingeniously utilised the discussion, always
> more or less under his direct control, as an edu-
> cational device for arraying precisely this body of
> propositions, deemed by him to be of some
> importance to his students at this stage of their
> classwork. The teaching skill exercised by such a
> tutor may be of a very high order, and the results
> gained may be of great educational value. To the
> extent that his students believe themselves to be
> participating in a genuinely open-ended dia-
> logue, however, they are being misled; and to the
> extent that he believes himself to be "conducting
> a discussion," he is misleading himself.

This balancing of genuine open-endedness with an awareness of what discussions can accomplish with some preparation is a delicate one. But preparing carefully for discussion is not the same as determining in advance its exact features; rather, preparing for discussion is a matter of ensuring that the free-ranging conversation that results is as informed, fair, and self-critical as possible. As a discussion leader you must be alert to the manipulative aspects of guided discussion. If you have a preconceived agenda, a specific idea of where you want the discussion to go, then you must acknowledge it fairly and fully. And if you decide to run your classes this way, don't make the mistake of thinking they are discussions in any meaningful sense.

### Be Clear About the Purposes of Discussion

Before deciding to use discussion methods for part or all of a course, you need to be quite clear in your own mind why you are doing this. Over thirty years ago, Brunner and others (1959) noted that discussion was often used for its own sake, regardless of its merits or suitability for particular pedagogic or curricular purposes. So think about why you're using discussion before you devote so much effort to it. The following intellectual, emotional, and social purposes seem to be some of the ones to which discussion is well suited.

*Intellectual Purposes*

*1. To Engage Students in Exploring a Diversity of Perspectives.* In discussion teachers encourage students to consider seriously the widely different interpretations made by various group members of the same, apparently objective, facts. In discussions one cannot skim through arguments and perspectives alternative to one's own—the physical presence of the proponents of these "inconvenient" views in the same room ensures this. Discussion participants are forced to take seriously the diversity of opinions and interpretations expressed on any one issue.

**2. To Assist Students in Discovering New Perspectives.** Discovering new perspectives involves entering other people's interpretive frameworks and assessing situations and events from unfamiliar points of view. Through listening carefully to other participants' contributions and through understanding the rationale informing arguments contrary to their own, students become more adept at seeing the world through unfamiliar eyes.

**3. To Emphasize the Complexity and Ambiguity of Issues, Topics, or Themes.** After good discussions, participants leave with more questions raised than answered. There is a sense that a topic is complex and contingent and requires more sustained study and reflection. Issues are opened and themes explored that complicate and qualify what was previously seen as closed or definitive.

**4. To Help Students Recognize the Assumptions Underlying Many of Their Habitual Ideas and Behaviors.** When discussion participants ask each other to support their statements and to explain their beliefs, students' underlying assumptions are revealed. Distinguishing between fact and opinion—or, rather, coming to realize that what one regards as facts are framed by the assumptions one holds—is a constant feature of a good discussion.

**5. To Increase Intellectual Agility.** In discussions we have to think on our feet. There is little chance to anticipate all possible objections to our point before we speak. So participating in discussions is intellectually hair-raising, since we risk having to defend our ideas against completely unanticipated arguments at the very time these arguments are offered to us. We have to try to answer requests for evidence, reasoning, and further information without the time for private reflection that we would normally devote to meeting such requests.

**6. To Encourage Active Listening.** A good part of discussion participation is devoted to listening carefully to others' ideas.

Attending to the expression of views that are complex and highly abstract or rambling, disconnected, and opaque is extremely demanding. To be required to attend seriously to these expressions and to try to make sense of them in terms of one's own experience and mental structures is difficult. But for people who are used to talking not listening and to having their voice heard rather than hearing others, this kind of active listening is one of the most valuable intellectual activities they can experience.

### Emotional Purposes

*1. To Increase Students' Affective Connections to a Topic.* Speaking about an idea, proposing an interpretation, or defending an argument are affective as well as cognitive actions. Doing these things tends to heighten students' sense of connection to and involvement with the discussion topic. The topic comes to have personal meaning as well as purely intellectual significance. Also, because discussion participation is such an emotional experience, it tends to arouse, sustain, or increase students' interest in a topic.

*2. To Show Students That They Are Heard, That Their Voices Matter, and That Their Experiences Are Valued.* Feeling that their ideas and beliefs mean something increases students' sense of self-worth and strengthens their self-confidence. Affirming students' sense of self-esteem is a powerful affective underpinning of all college teaching and is crucial to sustained learning. When people who are not used to having their ideas granted any public credibility find that they are being listened to carefully and seriously, this is an astoundingly powerful experience. It can precipitate major changes in their self-images, and the ripple effect may spill over into other aspects of their personal, occupational, and political lives.

### Social Purposes

*1. To Help Develop a Sense of Group Identity.* Discussion sessions are one way of increasing students' sense of connected-

ness to each other. Building a sense of group cohesion—a
supportive learning community—is especially important in
large-scale higher educational programs. An emotionally sustaining network of peers helps reduce the alienation and
isolation felt by students in programs dominated by mass
instruction and centrally produced materials.

2. *To Encourage Democratic Habits.* If run properly, discussion groups are true democratic laboratories. Depending on
the moral culture evolved to guide participants' interactions,
such groups are governed by democratic values such as freedom of expression, respect for minority opinion, tolerance of
diversity, and participatory involvement. The experience of
participating in groups where democracy is taken seriously is
a powerful one for students. It is just as powerful for teachers
to exercise civic courage (Giroux, 1983) by taking the reality
of democracy seriously in their classrooms.

Although flexibility and risk taking are crucial components of discussion, it is a mistake to think that discussions
are wholly spontaneous, free-ranging events. Good discussions
do not just happen. They usually result from some degree of
preplanning by those involved (teachers and students) around
a number of preparatory steps. Several of these are outlined
in the following paragraphs.

### Choose Discussion Topics Carefully

In framing your discussion sessions, make sure you choose
topics that are not too factual or uncontroversial. Choose
questions that cannot be answered by students during the
course of their preparatory reading and to which a number of
tenable, but markedly divergent, responses are possible. It is
better to present groups with questions to be answered rather
than with abstract questions. People can prepare much better
for a discussion on the question, "Does lecturing promote
retention of knowledge?" than for one on "The lecture as a
teaching method." It is also a good idea to guard against the
danger of what you thought would be an animated discussion

fizzling out after a few minutes of desultory conversation. Have available a reserve of alternate questions, possible themes, typical dilemmas, contentious issues, and provocative materials.

## Provide Preparatory Materials

Merely because people are gathered together for the purpose of discussion does not guarantee that anything worthwhile will occur. Discussions can quickly degenerate into non-communicative intolerance if participants merely exchange entrenched prejudices on the basis of mutual ignorance. So make sure that students share access to materials well before any meeting. In this way, they will have a common pool of concepts, ideas, factual information, and explanations to inform their participation. This reduces the risk of discussions meandering aimlessly along tributaries of irrelevance.

## Evolve Consensual Rules

Participant training is so crucial to success in discussions that the first session or sessions in a discussion-based course should be devoted to evolving procedural rules and codes of conduct to guide subsequent meetings. These rules of conduct should ensure that minority opinions are respected, that no one is allowed to dominate the group, that divergent views are allowed full and free expression, and that there is no pressure to reach premature and artificial solutions to problems posed. There can be rules set for the order in which participants can initiate new themes or respond to those already raised. There can be time limits set on members' contributions or a maximum number of contributions allowed.

You can approach this process in several ways. You can use a critical incident approach in which students describe their most memorable discussions and see whether any general rules about what makes for good discussions can be inferred from these descriptions. You can introduce examples of rules other groups have evolved and ask for opinions on these. My own preference is to begin a discussion-based course with an exercise designed to analyze students' past experiences of this method. I will say something like the following:

> Discussion is a difficult and emotional process so let's do what we can at the outset to improve the chances that our discussions will be valuable. First of all, think about the discussions you've been involved with that went well. What was it about these discussions that made them such good experiences for you? Then, think about the bad discussions and what made them so disappointing. Is there anything that emerges from both of these contexts to clarify what makes for a good discussion? Using this information, let's see what we can do to increase our chances that we'll avoid some of the pitfalls and enjoy some of the benefits of a good discussion.

As students talk about their experiences, the whole group goes through an inductive analysis of which general features ought to be encouraged and which ought to be dissuaded. As these general features are identified, I will ask the group how we can design specific rules to embody these. For example, if it's agreed that good discussions involve lots of people talking, then I'll ask how we can make sure that no one takes an unfair share of the conversation. Then we consider specific ways this general suggestion can be implemented. Should we place a time limit on individual contributions? Should we limit the number of contributions any participant can make in the whole session? Should we have a rule that a participant should wait until at least three other people have spoken before speaking again?

### Personalize Discussion Topics

Attempts to foster discussion of broad themes may well founder as a result of participants perceiving such themes to be unrelated to their own individual lives. This is particularly the case where the discussion of social and political issues is concerned. People frequently perceive themselves to be helpless in the face of overwhelming social forces. They regard their lives as relatively insignificant brush strokes when viewed against the background of the broad canvas of social change. So the connections between students' individual lives and wider changes—between the personal and political—is either wholly unfathomable or completely ignored.

If points of connection can be uncovered between students' experiences and broader themes or if students can be encouraged to imagine themselves in hypothetical situations and dilemmas and describe the reasons for these actions, then the exploration of broad themes becomes more immediate and charged with significance. Asking participants to think in these personalized ways about a general theme and perhaps to make a few brief notes on these reflections to consult during the discussion is an important preparatory step.

### Attend to the Group's Size

Group dynamics are an important factor in discussion. Opinions on the optimal size for interaction differ, but the consensus seems to be that somewhere between twelve and sixteen offers the best chance over a long period for provocative discussion. A group smaller than this is fine for a while, but after several meetings you may find that conversation has run dry, with members repeating themselves. A group larger than this can be too intimidating to those who find public speaking embarrassing. Yet the group is still large enough to be broken down into smaller combinations for small-group exercises. This is not a hard and fast rule, however, and a lot depends on the cultural conditioning of group members.

### Introduce Some Productive Dissonance

You should also be aware of the tendency for many college discussion groups to display a remarkable homogeneity of opinion on many issues. Because of the similarity of students'

backgrounds and experiences in some institutions, it is sometimes hard to assemble groups containing members with divergent outlooks. This does vary, of course, from community to
community. The composition of groups in colleges that draw
from their surrounding multiethnic, multiclass communities
will be different from that of groups in colleges drawing from
communities that are economically and ethnically mono-
chrome.

If your students exhibit interpretive unanimity, then
you have to find ways of shaking them out of this. Before the
discussions begin, think about how you can disturb their comfortable, settled worldviews in ways that stimulate rather than
threaten. In your lectures you can argue strongly and clearly
for views that contradict majority opinion. In the preparatory
reading for the discussion, you can ask students to review
arguments critical of dominant cultural values. You can try
some of the role reversal or critical debate techniques outlined
in the chapter on simulations and role plays. You can try
Kennedy's (1990) technique of ideological analysis, in which
students identify moments in their life histories when they
were aware of a disjunction between their own instincts and
feelings and the dominant ideologies around them.

As Daloz (1986) writes, one of the most important
things discussion leaders can do is to "toss little bits of disturbing information in their students' paths, little facts and
observations, theories and interpretations—cow plops on the
road to truth—that raise questions about their students' current world views and invite them to entertain alternatives, to
close the dissonance, accommodate their structures, *think*
afresh" (p. 223). There are times "when a good dose of confusion is exactly what a student may need" (p. 224), since "an
appropriate dose of conflicting or counterintuitive information can raise questions about the student's givens" (p. 126).
This is never more true than when you are dealing with a
group whose members possess a marked homogeneity of opinion. Unless you find ways of producing some stimulating
dissonance and of jolting them out of the ruts of their comfortable worldviews, you may as well forget about holding

discussions at all. There is no point in using this method if it only helps students settle more deeply into these ruts.

## Be Careful About Grading Procedures

In order to encourage students to participate in discussions, teachers sometimes award a percentage of a final course grade for participation. This certainly will motivate students to contribute, but it can produce unfortunate side effects. If students know that 20 or 30 percent of their grade will be awarded for their class participation, the pressure on them to contribute for contribution's sake becomes irresistible. This may result in lively, animated discussions, but the contemplative interludes of silence so essential to the praxis of learning will be made almost impossible.

Grading for discussion participation can be a good idea, provided that what is meant by "participation" is clearly defined beforehand. I would suggest doing several things, including broadening the definition of participation to include performing silent group roles such as those of recorder or summarizer. I would also include as examples of discussion participation the trouble students take to find preparatory reading materials suitable for upcoming topics, or the act of bringing to the group a salient article, chapter, or piece of information as a follow-up to a previous discussion. Under the heading of participation, I would include the keeping of learning journals or the compilation of critical incident reports. If someone who was too shy or confused to speak while a discussion was in progress had an insight about the topic after the session had finished and then wrote this down and xeroxed it for other members of the group, this would seem to me an example of participation. Finally, I would give examples and case studies of effective participation at the beginning of the course that emphasize the contributions of students who called for periods of silence in the session. Talking approvingly of students who are able to recognize when people need to stop talking and spend a few minutes in quiet reflection sends a strong message to shy and quiet students about the nature of participation.

≈≈≈ CHAPTER EIGHT

# Facilitating
# Discussions

Any guidelines for conducting discussions must, of necessity, be speculative. By its very nature discussion is unpredictable. If we knew what was going to happen in a session, it would cease to be a discussion in any meaningful sense. Every discussion group is a unique constellation of personalities, a universe unto itself. How these individuals will perceive and react to a leader's comments or other group members' contributions cannot possibly be anticipated in advance.

During discussions you will have to make innumerable contextual decisions. The rest of this chapter explores some of the problematic decisions most typically faced by discussion leaders. But don't think that discussions are activities in which you can anticipate and prepare for all eventualities. They are both glorious and frustrating in their sprawling messiness, and no matter how often you use discussions, you will never reach a point where you can't be knocked sideways by some totally unexpected comment or behavior.

## Getting Discussions Started

The first minutes of discussion are often fairly embarrassing as teachers ask a series of questions, try to cajole the students into responding, and then end up answering the questions themselves. To avoid this kind of embarrassment, you can adapt the critical incident technique to a discussion setting by asking participants to begin the session by recalling an event in their own lives that connects to the topic under review. After three or four people have spoken about these events, you can ask other students to identify commonalities and differences in these accounts.

If using critical incidents is inappropriate, you can try reading out a contentious statement by an authority figure on the topic concerned and ask students to discuss what is right and wrong with this statement. Or, you can mention one or two provocative key words associated with the topic and ask for group members to do some free associating on the meaning of these for them. It may be a good idea for you to assign roles beforehand to different participants, so that two or three different students have the responsibility for introducing the chief contentious issues and the major disagreements in perspective at the start of each discussion period. As these students are speaking, other group members are asked to listen carefully for opinions masquerading as facts, for unacknowledged biases, for contradictions, and for errors and then to speak about these once the initial presentations have ended.

## Dealing with the Overly Talkative

Groups will always differ in the degree to which different members contribute, and this should not be a cause for undue concern. However, there are times when one or two members are so confident, articulate, and convinced of their correctness, or are simply used to dominating conversations of which they are a·part, that this becomes a problem. They may take up an unfair proportion of discussion time, exclude those with less verbal acuity, and intimidate those who feel their opinions have little merit to begin with.

If groups have taken the time to evolve fair rules of discussion, this problem is usually more easily dealt with. You or, better still, another group member can remind the person who is talking too much of the rules about the frequency or length of contributions. The person giving this reminder and the person receiving it will both feel better about the situation if this reminder is framed in the context of previously agreed-upon rules. But no matter how you try to prevent this from happening, sooner or later you will come up against the problem of the overly talkative group member. Of all the questions regarding discussion leadership that are raised at teaching workshops I have given, the largest single category concerns this situation. In my experience, five responses seem useful, and I would suggest trying them in the order presented here.

First, I would suggest taking the student aside and saying something along the following lines: "Look, I know you learn best by contributing, and I appreciate the eagerness with which you're willing to pitch in to get discussions going, but I'm worried that with your confidence and your speed of articulation you may be unwittingly stifling the contributions of others who are less confident. I know you don't mean to do this, but you are so quick and assured in your contributions that some group members are getting into the habit of letting you do the speaking for them because that's so much easier than talking for themselves. In the interests of their learning, I wonder if you could try and exercise a bit more self-restraint with respect to the length and frequency of your contributions?"

Note that the tone of this suggestion is respectful and acknowledges the student's contribution. It is a real mistake to adopt at the outset a truculent tone in which you accuse the student of destroying the group process. Instead, try to appeal to the student's commitment to improving the quality of discussion interaction. This makes the person feel respected and consulted in a collegial way, rather than disciplined like an errant child.

How you phrase your request will depend partly on your perception of the person's reasons for speaking so much. Is it because of a passionate enthusiasm for the topic or because of a desire to dominate situations? After you have voiced your request, you can see what effect it has during the next couple of meetings. If nothing changes, then I would suggest a second strategy of specifying in precise behavioral terms exactly what you would like the person to do. Sometimes this can be done concurrent with the first step, but I prefer to think of it as the second possible response. It may be that after an initial conversation with the person concerned things may improve so much that this second, more specific, request is unnecessary.

As part of this second response, I ask that the person concerned do two specific things. Neither of these will preclude the student contributing to the discussion but both will increase the chances of others speaking. First I say, "When you want to say something, will you count to ten before speaking? If, by then, no one else has said anything, then feel free to pitch in." Second, I say, "When you have spoken in the group, can you wait for at least three other group members to say something before you make your next contribution? You can waive this if someone asks you a direct question, or if they want you to elaborate on something you've just said, but otherwise I'd like you to try following this general rule." Saying these things does not silence the talkative person or ban any and all contributions, but it does give two easily remembered rules of thumb for discussion participation.

These first two responses to this problem do have, as Rogers (1989, p. 190) points out, the danger of "suggesting a conspiracy between yourself and your specially clever student, with both of you agreeing to patronize the less fortunate slower people." As with so many decisions associated with teaching, it is essentially a trade-off between appearing to generate a patronizing, private conspiracy and having the student continue to dominate discussion in a way which does great harm to the learning of others. My feeling is that it is worth running the risk of seeming to be conspiring for the benefits that restraining the person's behavior will bring.

Whatever happens, it is very important that you acknowledge to the overly talkative student that you appreciate the efforts he or she is making to follow your suggestions. Thank this person for exercising a self-restraint and acknowledge that you know that this is difficult since it goes against the student's usual style. Point out how many more people are speaking or how someone who hasn't spoken before has made a contribution. Make a connection between the talkative student's self-denial and the increased quality of discussion participation.

The third strategy for dealing with this situation is more complicated and involves more effort than the first two. It entails assigning to group members a number of roles and functions on a rotating basis. These roles can be those of recorder, summarizer, proposer, opposer, detective of unacknowledged biases, suggester of further questions, and so on. Performing these roles requires periods of silence on the part of those playing them. By rotating the role of recorder (whose duty it is to make a full record of the group's deliberations), summarizer (who chips in every twenty minutes with a three-minute summary of what's been said in the last discussion segment), and detective (who listens carefully for a period to several comments and then speaks about the unacknowledged biases heard in people's comments), you ensure that the overly talkative person is silently pursuing a function on behalf of the group for at least some of the time.

It is important that you rotate these roles fairly. Always asking the talkative person to be the recorder who stays silent for the whole session is blatant and unfair. But no one can complain about periodically being silent if this role is required regularly of all group members and this role is central to the quality of the group's discussion.

The main danger associated with this response to the problem of overly talkative students is that it is a bit like shutting the stable door after the horse has bolted. Suddenly shifting the conduct of discussion procedure to assign group roles in the way described can seem like a rather exaggerated response. Of course, if you begin discussions requiring that participants regularly perform these roles, this danger is removed. But most teachers who run into this problem do so because they have decided that establishing such roles at the beginning will do more harm than good where generating interaction is concerned.

If none of the three responses I have already described appears to have any effect on the situation, then I suggest that you think about raising this as a problem with the whole group. This is a dramatic step and is generally not necessary. But when the talkative student has an unusually strong personality, and when the other group members refuse to try and control this person, then this head-on approach may be unavoidable.

When you do decide to make this a group problem (rather than one involving only you and the student concerned), try to avoid making the person involved into a scapegoat. If you have reached the stage where you're considering this fourth response, then the other members cannot fail to have noticed what's happening. Begin by talking about the fact that the group—rather than the individual student—has a problem. Ask if anyone has suggestions why so many people seem unwilling to contribute to discussions. Point out that someone who talks a lot can't be blamed for doing so if no one else intervenes. Ask group members why they are, in effect, abdicating their own responsibility for learning to one particularly confident, articulate, knowledgeable person.

These are all hard things for teachers to do, particularly those who, like myself, much prefer affirmation over confrontation. Before such occasions my heart pounds so hard that I feel it's about to burst out of my chest, my hands drip what seem like buckets of sweat, and I speak in a brittle, stammering tone, betraying my nervousness. But sometimes you have to initiate these uncomfortable confrontations for the broader educational good of other students, even if you know that they, and you, would much rather avoid such distressing episodes.

Of course, like all the other strategies mentioned so far, this one can also fail completely. If so, you're probably no worse off than before, and you may be slightly better off because the situation has now been publicly acknowledged. The danger with this fourth response is that, if handled badly, you may seem to be haranguing the group for their laziness or battling one particularly strong person for leadership of the group. So you must always critically consider your own actions in this situation and search your motives to ensure, as far as you can, that the confrontation you initiate is not about your desire to always be seen in control of the group.

Finally, you may find yourself in a position where you either have to ask the person to withdraw from the group (which is often illegal or impossible because of precedent) or abandon discussion as a method. The latter course of action isn't as disastrous or defeatist as it sounds. It may be that you were wrong to use discussion in the first place for the outcomes you intended or for the students you are working with. By using small-group exercises, simulations, role plays, lectures, and independent study projects, you can give students a rich and rounded educational experience without ever using discussion. In any case, abandoning discussion may be a shrewd strategic withdrawal. After a break, the dynamics of the group may have altered sufficiently for you to feel that you can reintroduce this method.

### Encouraging Silent Members

In my experience, dealing with silent members is much less of a problem than dealing with overly talkative members. The right to silence should be acknowledged in discussion just as much as the right to speak. There is no point in forcing someone to speak if this only results in his or her embarrassment at being singled out as an unsatisfactory group member or if what is said in consequence is a nervous jumble of non sequiturs. Also, we must be wary of equating silence with mental inertia. As was discussed in Chapter Four, episodes of silent speculation are crucial to interpretation, to attempts to make meaning out of new ideas or facts. Early on in the life of a discussion group you need to make clear that talking for talking's sake will not be rewarded and that silence is not something to be avoided at all costs.

Bearing this in mind, I often begin discussion sessions with a general comment along the following lines:

I know that speaking in discussions is a nerve-wracking thing and that your fear of making public fools of yourselves can inhibit you to the point of nonparticipation. I, myself, feel very nervous as a discussion participant and spend a lot of my time carefully rehearsing my contributions so as not to look like an idiot when I finally speak. So please don't feel that you have to speak in order to gain my approval or to show me that you're a diligent student. It's quite acceptable not to say anything in the session, and there'll be no presumption of failure on your part. I don't equate your silence with mental inertia. Obviously I hope you will want to say something and speak up, but I don't want you to do this just for the sake of appearances.

Saying something like this often produces a collective sigh of relief and sometimes the overly diffident relax enough to actually contribute. Many people have come up to me at the end of a session to say how much they appreciated my opening remarks. So, in my view, equating your skill as a discussion leader with ensuring that everyone speaks is mistaken. In Rogers (1989, p. 189) words, "Not all discussions need to be noisy or obviously vigorous to be educationally valuable. A good discussion may be quiet, apparently low-key, with a lot of thoughtful silences."

If you are worried about silent members, there are two options you can consider. First, you can try assigning roles to participants on a rotating basis much as was described in the previous section. Sooner or later everyone has to adopt roles such as detective, summarizer, proposer, and opposer that require them to speak. Doing this may be painful for them, but they can take comfort in the fact that having performed this role once it will be some time before it comes round again. Also, it is important to their self-esteem for them to feel that they are fully participating group members. Performing mostly silent but important roles such as recorder lets them feel comfortable with their mostly silent participation. Second, you can ask group members to keep a learning journal—a log of "insights gained from discussion"—that they will submit to you regularly. By reading this you can verify that silent members are intellectually engaged in the discussion despite their reticence. The detail with which this journal is kept can be one component of any grade, or percentage of a grade, awarded for discussion participation.

### Reducing Analytical Confusion

Often a sense of bewilderment settles on discussion participants as, in a short period of time, several members make points that are at best only tenuously connected and at worst wholly divergent. It is not at all uncommon to find oneself ten minutes into a discussion characterized by a rapid succession of non sequiturs. Themes overlap rapidly, and then one member places a wholly different interpretation on a contribution than was originally intended by its speaker and introduces what seems like a succession of irrelevant associations. The conversation zigzags, doubles back, and leaps forward without any apparent fluidity or connection and quickly degenerates into mutual confusion.

   This will, to some degree, always happen and that is part of the unpredictable joy of discussion. The best way to keep it from getting out of hand is to select one or two group members to summarize after each fifteen- to twenty-minute discussion period. This means that after every fifteen to twenty minutes of discussion participants stop talking while they listen to one or two summaries by noncontributors of what has been said so far. I advocate two summaries because one person may have lost touch with what has been said.

   Having listened to these summaries, which is something like listening to an edited tape of their interactions, students can then be asked to choose two or three of the main themes presented in the summary to pursue in the next fifteen- to twenty-minute period of the discussion. This strategy has two advantages. First, people become aware that they may not really be listening to what others are saying because they are pursuing their own intellectual agenda. Second, people have to focus their attention on a limited number of themes in the next stage of the discussion.

## Avoiding Definitive Summaries

To linear, convergent thinkers the open-endedness of discussions can be intensely frustrating. They expect to learn "the answer," "the truth," or "what's on the test." The idea of multiplistic interpretations, of exploring the same issue from a variety of perspectives, is resisted strongly by those students who wish to view the discussion leader as the ultimate source of authority, the fount of intellectual wisdom.

To be in a position of such ascribed omniscience is embarrassing to some teachers and profoundly satisfying to others, but it is always inimical to discussion learning. If participants feel that their contributions are merely rehearsals, courteously observed formalities, before the leader lays down the truth in the form of a closing summary, then they will never participate in discussion with any genuine sense of honest searching or conviction. So as a discussion leader, you must avoid the habit of "giving the sense of the meeting" at the end of a discussion.

Nothing is more guaranteed to reduce one's belief in the value of discussion (and here I speak from experience as a participant) than hearing a leader pronounce at the end of a discussion, "Well, I think we're all agreed that these are the main points that have emerged today" and then to listen with astonishment as the leader presents a version of the discussion that seems to be entirely different than the one in which you've just participated. If you want to bring some sense of closure to discussions, you can ask one or two of the discussion participants to give their summaries of where they think the discussion has been. Alternatively, you can ask one or two students to list the unanswered questions they think have been raised by the discussion and the unresolved issues they feel are most in need of further study. This sends the strong message that intellectual inquiry is continuous and that discussion participants have as much responsibility for its conduct as does the leader.

## Protecting Minority Viewpoints

Discussion groups, like any other groups, develop recognizable cultures focused upon what are seen as majority beliefs and dominant values. Discussion leaders have a responsibility to ensure that the spread of acceptable opinion does not narrow to the point where divergent, minority viewpoints are regarded as deviant.

As discussion leader you can guard against the creeping tyranny of the majority in several ways. You can make sure that the minority viewpoint is allowed full expression by supporting a student who offers an opinion that several other students immediately discard. An especially strong message is sent to students if you deliberately encourage the expression of opinions critical to those you are known to hold. If no member of the group feels courageous enough to voice such opinions, you can play devil's advocate with your own interpretations and present the best arguments you can muster against the beliefs you have just expressed. Groups who admire their teachers have a dangerous tendency to try to quiet members who voice opinions critical of those teachers, and unless teachers are aware of this possibility, the prospects for free and open exchange can be seriously damaged.

## Accepting the Emotionality of Discussion

As anyone who has been burned in the fiery crucible of pedagogic experience knows, discussions can be intensely competitive battlegrounds. They can also be the forum in which people let down their defenses to reveal aspects of their personalities that they have previously regarded as highly personal and private. Groups can become bitterly factional in a very short time, with members spending their energy replaying aggressive patterns of interaction fixed in the first few meetings. Or, they can become cohesive units, characterized by deeply felt bonds of commitment, respect, and obligation. Students weep tears of joy, frustration, hostility, and relief.

It is not uncommon for me to leave a discussion session feeling completely drained, emotionally wrung out. I am tired, exhilarated, depressed, puzzled, and excited all at the same time. I find it difficult to talk to anyone and like to shut myself away in privacy for an hour or two. If the session has been held in the evening, I take at least two to three hours to wind down. At times like these, I watch the videotapes of the "David Letterman" show that have been piling up at home.

Teachers who use discussion need to be prepared for the emotional disarray it causes. They need to remember that many of their students are probably feeling the same way, though this may not be immediately evident. Boredom is readily detected (the snoring gives it away), but many students have learned the lesson that overt displays of emotion within the formal classroom environment are to be avoided. Nevertheless, apparently placid conversations may catch fire without warning, and the most stoic participants may sometimes display strong emotions. So don't be surprised when you leave a discussion feeling taut and stretched.

## The Significance of Discussion

Participating in discussion—in the collaborative effort to find meaning in and to make sense of our experience—calls for courage and hard work on the part of students and teachers. It requires that the distinction between learners and leaders be forgotten as much as is humanly possible, although it is naive to think it can ever be completely erased. I remember well my own skepticism at teachers who declared that their discussion groups were leaderless and democratic, yet who subtly controlled the interactions and judged the value of each person's contribution through the award of end-of-semester grades. But it is possible for teachers to demonstrate through their actions—particularly through their readiness to admit to error and to invite the same critical scrutiny of their own ideas and contributions as they do of others—that an atmosphere of openness, trust, and confidentiality prevails.

When conducted authentically, discussion is not an easy, soft option. It is intellectually taxing and emotionally unsettling. It requires participants to attend carefully to what others are saying. It places the responsibility for the success of the activity in students' hands as much as in the teacher's expertise, for even the most animatedly enthusiastic and well-informed leader can do little if students steadfastly refuse to respond.

Students have to present their ideas as clearly as possible, respond thoughtfully to others' reactions to these, and interpret other students' ideas, which may be expressed in highly personalized, ambiguous ways. And they have to do all this in an atmosphere that may be highly competitive and without a chance to rehearse contributions so that they come out smoothly and confidently. Small wonder, then, that participating in the sprawling, wayward, emotionally charged activity we know as discussion represents for many students and teachers their most memorable college experience.

# CHAPTER NINE

# Using Simulations
# and Role Playing

Both simulations and role plays explore dimensions other than the purely cognitive, and both are affectively based (Lewis, 1986). They reproduce within the artificial classroom environment the visceral flow of feeling as it is experienced outside this setting. In simulations and role plays, students feel the heightened sensations associated with real-life dilemmas, decisions, and problems. Because these exercises parallel actual experience, they tend to be infused with a drama and passion that make them stand out in sharp emotional relief when they are described within the pages of students' journals and learning logs.

Participating in simulations and role plays involves students in crossing psychomotor, affective, and cognitive domains and calls upon them to be alert to a wide range of sensory stimuli. Because of the emotional tone of such exercises, they often engage students much more directly and vividly than do more reflective activities such as reading or listening. Because this kind of learning involves the whole person—intellect, feeling, and bodily senses—it tends to be experienced more deeply and remembered longer.

The realism of many simulations and role plays also means that they are perceived by students as being of genuine significance and relevance, and this is one reason why teachers should consider using them. The insights derived from these experiential methods tend to be etched much more firmly onto people's perceptual filters and structures of understanding. So if you want your students to gain a strong visceral connection to their learning, if you want them to regard their learning activities as having immediate relevance to their lives outside the classroom, and if you want this learning to be recalled long after it has happened, then you should consider using the methods discussed in this chapter.

### Simulations

Simulations involve students in re-creating within the classroom some of the dilemmas, crises, and problems they have experienced or are experiencing outside. Alternatively they involve them in working through imagined, hypothetical situations that are recognizably close to those occurring in their lives. To be most effective (that is, to engage students most directly and vividly), simulation exercises must have the ring of truth. They should feel authentic.

Participating in authentic simulations, in valid reconstructions of recognizable crises, helps to develop students' contextual awareness. As students in a simulation exercise propose, debate, and make judgments about alternative courses of action suggested by different people, they can hardly fail to realize what a wide range of idiosyncratic interpretations are made of the same "objective" facts by different team members, nor can they fail to be struck by the diversity of solutions offered. Participants in simulations also tend to be made more aware of their own assumptions since they have to respond to each other's requests for explanations and justifications to support the various responses proposed.

In the following paragraphs, I reproduce and discuss two simulation exercises of my own design. I am not offering them as specific exercises for you to employ directly, they are far too much a product of my own work for that. But they do illustrate some of the general features of simulation exercises.

*Crisis Decision Simulation.* The first simulation is an example of a crisis decision simulation, so-called because it requires participants to respond immediately to an imagined crisis without the benefit of clear guidelines concerning what is morally right or culturally appropriate.

### *Crisis Decision Simulation: Invidious Choices*

Form into groups of four.

You are members of a college committee appointed to award discretionary merit payments to faculty. This year three nominations have been received (the letters of nomination are provided). One nomination is from the college president, who has proposed that a certain professor receive the award for her effort in securing a major grant for the college. As a result of her effort, several faculty have been able to take time off from teaching to pursue their own research. A second nomination is from a group of students who wish to honor a junior, untenured professor whom they regard as an exemplary teacher. A third nomination comes from a group of faculty who want to recognize a colleague whose writings and outside speaking have brought considerable prestige and prominence to the college as a whole.

You are meeting as a committee to consider these nominations, and you have forty minutes to come up with your recommendation. Whom do you choose and why?

The best results from this exercise will accrue if three of you choose to argue as strongly and unequivocally as you can for each of these three nominations. In other words, one of you should argue for the faculty member who has secured the major grant, one should argue for the exemplary instructor, and one should argue for the person whose writings and speaking have brought prestige to the college as a whole. The fourth person should play the role of uncommitted participant who could be swayed to support any of the three nominations.

Incidentally, as you choose one of these four roles, I would advise you to support the nomination you most disagree with. This will provide a useful example of the benefits of the role-reversal technique, particularly how it can help you appreciate perspectives with which you are unfamiliar.

The most useful aspect of this simulation, and the major reason why I would use it, is the extent to which it prompts three processes of critical thinking—contextual awareness, imaginative speculation, and assumption analysis. Students increase their contextual awareness through recognizing how antithetical actions proposed by different team members are often contextually determined, reflecting participants' own biographies, values, and cultures. They engage in imaginative speculation by trying to generate alternatives to the choices that have been forced upon them by the exercise. The exercise is called "Invidious Choices" since no matter whom they choose, they will offend some important body of opinion. Assumption analysis occurs in three ways. First, participants will talk about the assumptions underlying the nomination of each of the three candidates. Second, they will point out to each other the assumptions they feel underlie each other's proposed actions. Third, through the questioning of their own proposals by other group members, they will be made to examine those assumptions that inform their choices. Related benefits from this kind of simulation are helping participants become more aware of group dynamics, improving their team membership abilities, and sensitizing them to the stress of having to make difficult choices, in quick time, under great pressure—surely a generic imperative of adult life.

*Training Simulation.* The second simulation is an example of a training simulation. Training simulations are designed to give participants the chance to experience and begin to resolve a problem, crisis, or dilemma typically faced in their lives. As a result, these simulations are best suited to courses in which students are being prepared for the demands of a particularly stressful situation. They are commonly found, for example, in teacher training, social work preparation, counseling education, family therapy, and training sessions devoted to preparing people for voluntary action, community initiatives, and political action. Recently, no aspiring political figure has failed to participate in a training simulation designed to develop expertise in performing well in front of television cameras.

The following simulation is designed for college teachers and concerns a situation that I, and many others, have experienced to some degree.

### Training Simulation: The Joker

Form yourselves into groups of three. You will do this exercise in small groups and then reconvene as a large group at the end of the exercise to share your experiences and insights.

### Background

You are three teachers who are coteaching a class. Because you believe it is important that students be exposed to a variety of perspectives, personalities, and teaching styles, you have arranged to alternate responsibility for leading group discussions. Consequently, each one of you sees the class only once every three weeks, and each of you teaches your sessions alone.

### Situation

Last week you each received a verbal complaint and a letter from some students about Stephen, one of your students. The focus of these complaints is that Stephen (a white American in his mid-twenties) consistently makes ethnic and sexist jokes in class that several members find offensive. He also uses humor to insult teachers in a way that disturbs some students, and these learners feel that Stephen's wisecracks are diverting too much of the class's attention.

The verbal complaint has been made separately to each

of you by a young Japanese female student who is so distressed about the situation (and her response to it) that she
begs all of you to keep her identity anonymous. The letter
has been signed by five of the group of seventeen students in
the class, and it makes reference to the general need for
teachers to monitor more carefully sexist and racist remarks
in class. Stephen's name is not mentioned, but from your
own observations and from the verbal complaint, you are
pretty sure that he is the reason for the letter.

Today, matters have been brought to a head by two
events. First, a student has left a videotape in each of your
mail boxes that was made during a class exercise one of you
ran last week. The video was made at your request by a student who was to submit it to you for editing so that you
could then distribute it to group members as part of a training session on group dynamics and discussion that is to be
held sometime in the future. You all watched this video today
and were distressed to see the young woman who has com-
plained to you weeping quietly at the edge of the camera
range after a wisecrack by Stephen.

The second way in which matters have been brought to
a head is by a report from one of you who has just finished
teaching this week's class. This teacher is sure that there is a
real tension in the room, though no student has made any
explicit mention of a problem during your session. Stephen
appeared quite unaffected by the tension detected and seemed
happy, relaxed, and apparently oblivious to any effects his
behavior might be having.

*Your Task*

You have the chance to see the video of the class exercise and
to read the letter from the five students. You are also supplied
with a copy of an extract from an essay one of you has
received as a homework assignment from Stephen that is peppered with his humorous asides. On the basis of this information and drawing on your previous experience with jokers,
the three of you have to decide what to do next time the class
meets.

*Time Alloted*

1 to 10 minutes: Watch the videotape.
10 to 20 minutes: Read the letter from the five students and the extract from Stephen's homework assignment.
20 to 50 minutes: Discuss what to do next time the class meets.
50 to 60 minutes: Break—coffee, tea, and reflection.
60 to 90 minutes: Small groups report on their discussions, describe their suggested responses, and give the reasons for these.

*Resources*

Video of class exercise
Letter of complaint
Extract from Stephen's homework assignment

This simulation is an artificially heightened presentation of a situation—the student who never seems able to make a serious comment and whom you feel has designated himself or herself the class joker—that is fairly common but that rarely plays itself out in the dramatic manner depicted in the exercise. It is possible to extend this simulation even further by setting up a role play in which Stephen (a role that I, as simulation designer, would probably play) meets with the group of team teachers to discuss their request for him to leave the class. This role play can be set up with one of the small groups involved in the exercise while the rest of the class observe and then contribute to the debriefing and analysis after the role play has ended. The exercise can also be shortened or lengthened and the amount of information available to participants can be varied.

## Using Simulations

Four points need to be made with regard to the educational use of simulations such as the two already outlined. First, the debriefing and analysis that follows the simulation is as important as the simulation itself. Allow plenty of time for groups to report on their contrasting responses to simulations, for them to analyze the reasoning processes that led them to their decisions, and for them to reflect on alternative responses they might have made. A good rule is to allow as much time for analysis as the simulation exercise took to play itself out.

Second, simulations never stay exactly the same. Not only do different groups respond in surprising, unpredictable ways to the same exercises but also the simulation instructions and resources are honed and refined through continual use (Greenblatt, 1988). Each time you use a simulation you are subjecting it to a form of reality testing by having your students gauge its accuracy and credibility against their own experiences. So be ready to add information, delete characters, adjust the timing, change the tasks, and make other alterations to the exercise the more frequently it is used (Jones, 1985, 1988). Pay particular attention to comments from participants in the analysis session about the unreality or inauthenticity of aspects of the exercise.

Third, it will be obvious from these examples that simulations are not a way for teachers to get out of the hard work of teaching. They are not soft options, and they are neither quick nor dirty. They take a long time to think through and prepare. For the joker simulation, one has to prepare two documents (the letter and the homework extract) and a videotape (though this could be dropped if time and resources did not allow), make constant alterations to these, provide clear instructions to participants, monitor groups' activities, and run the debriefing. So simulations are not serendipitous events. In fact, since planners of simulations have to try to anticipate multiple eventualities prompted by their exercises, they spend as much if not more time planning these than preparing lectures.

Finally, simulations should not be used if you feel uncertain about, unsure of, or unfamiliar with the material that is the focus of the exercise. Although simulations are carefully planned, there is always an open-ended element to the ways they play themselves out. Using them is not for the fainthearted. So unless you feel you know your area well enough to respond to all kinds of unpredictable eventualities—to be able to think on your feet and respond quickly to unforeseen outcomes—you should wait before trying simulations.

## Role Play

Role play focuses on investigating new perspectives, that is, helping people explore the perceptual filters and interpretive structures that shape how other people see the world (Milroy, 1982; Van Ments, 1989). Doing this is complicated and intimidating. When successful, however, it integrates cognitive and affective dimensions of learning in a powerful way. Through role play we gain a greater appreciation for the particular mix of thought processes, habitual reflexes, assumptions, unquestioned attitudes, perceptions, and emotions informing people's actions in crises (Shaw, Corsini, Blake, and Mouton, 1982).

Role play is also a technique that can help prepare us for emotionally charged, complex crises we may face at some time in our lives. It can assist, in however contrived or artificial a way, in our living through the confusion induced by ambiguous situations in which no clear, correct response is evident. Although it can never prepare us fully for the experiential reality of dealing with anger, bitterness, interpersonal conflict, or the pain of divided loyalties, it can help us be less thrown when these emotions actually arise.

When preparing and conducting role plays, several guidelines are important. I shall examine each of these in turn.

*Research the Scene Well.* If the scene to be played is not convincing to its players, if it lacks plausibility, then the value of the exercise is destroyed. So it is important for teachers to research the typical crises and problems facing their students. One useful approach is to use a critical incident technique. The following is one I have used in preparing staff development efforts, including role plays, for teachers:

*Critical Incident: Teaching Problems*

Think back over the past six months of your life as a teacher. Identify the incident that caused you the greatest discomfort, difficulty, or anxiety—the event that made you speculate about giving up teaching. Write down a brief description of the incident, making sure that you give details of where and when it occurred, who was involved, and what it was about the incident that caused you such anxiety. (Please don't reveal personal identities—use job titles or descriptions of roles instead.)

Using a critical incident like this lets you gain an accurate record of the real concerns, problems, and dilemmas of the teachers surveyed. Because these incident descriptions are private, teachers feel more comfortable about revealing anxieties and problems that would be embarrassing for them to admit to their colleagues in a public setting. Also, since critical incidents focus on specific events, teachers are less likely to reply using conventional clichés that come quickly and easily to mind.

By administering a critical incident like the one above to several of the likely participants in the role play before the exercise takes place, you stand a much better chance of designing a role-play scenario that is grounded in deeply felt and viscerally experienced concerns. But there are also other ways of finding out about the concerns of participants in role plays you are designing. If you have the time, and if your students agree, you can observe them in the actual situations around which the role play will be structured. You can interview students directly or talk to people who will not be in the role play but who live and work in the same settings as your participants do. You can read secondary accounts (if they are available) of what it's like to live and work in these settings. But none of these approaches, in my view, is as simply administered and liable to produce such accurate information as the critical incident technique.

*Get the Exercise Reviewed.* If possible, ask one or two people to review your role-play instructions. By using the critical incident information, you stand a good chance of creating a role play that will be experienced as truthful and familiar to participants. But there is always the chance that in your interpretation of the critical incident responses, in the way you describe the chronology of events, in the inclusion of a contextually inappropriate piece of behavior, or in the way you've set up the scene you've unwittingly damaged the credibility of the exercise.

You may also have unwittingly fallen foul of one of the two most common pitfalls in writing role plays—giving too much or too little detail. Giving too much detail cramps participants' style and inhibits the freedom to improvise that is so necessary for full involvement in a scene. Students feel they are following a script prepared by someone else rather than creating their own authentic representation of a real-life event from which they can learn something important. Giving too little information means people cannot get a sense of the characters they are playing, and thus their behaviors in the exercise feel like blind guesses rather than intuitive but informed actions. So submitting your role-play design to the scrutiny of people who've experienced something like the events described, and whose opinion you can trust, is a useful form of pilot testing the exercise.

*Explain Your Purposes Clearly.* Role plays are emotionally charged events and require a lot of students. This is particularly so with those (like me) who are self-conscious and embarrassed at "acting" in front of a group. If you're going to ask people to put themselves through such an intense and uncomfortable experience, they deserve to know exactly why you think this is so important for them to endure and what benefits they can expect to derive from the experience.

*Cast the Exercise Sensitively.* Roles are not randomly assigned in a role-play exercise. You need to ask yourself several important questions about how you will cast students in different roles. First, will you allow students to choose whether to be observers or players? If you decide you want to use a role-play exercise at all, then I believe you should use the technique several times so that everyone in the group is asked to be a player and an observer at least once.

Second, you have to decide whether to cast players in roles with which they are familiar or whether to ask them to play against type. If you want to encourage them to explore different perspectives, then you should cast people against type, since this is a very dramatic way of helping someone see a situation as another sees it. If you want to help students resolve a problem they are constantly facing or explore whether their habitual actions in such situations are the most useful for what they want to achieve, then casting to type is advisable. This should also be done if you want students to generate and explore novel responses to commonly experienced crises. For these purposes it will be most helpful to participants in role plays if they are playing roles close enough to their own contexts for their actions to be seen as recognizable and felt as authentic and for them to be able to transfer the insights they gained from the exercise into their own real-life circumstances.

*Give Clear Instructions to Observers.* Just as important as making sure that the actors in a role play are well briefed is paying attention to the clarity of your instructions to observers. After all, they are supposed to be learning just as much from watching a role play, albeit in a different way, as the actors are from playing out their roles. Tell observers what you want them to be looking for, upon whom each individual observer should concentrate (if this is appropriate), and how observers can gain as much from a role play as the more active participants.

In particular, observers should be told how to structure their comments to the actors during the debriefing and analysis session. They should be asked to accentuate the positive in the scene by first identifying the actions of the players they felt were insightful and sensitive before making more critical comments. When making criticisms, they should acknowledge the complexity of the situation in which the actors found themselves and, if possible, they should follow their criticisms with their own suggestions about the actions they would have taken themselves. They should be made aware of the emotionally charged nature of role play (this is one reason why students should be both observers and actors at different times) and warned of the likelihood of their criticisms producing a reaction of surprisingly intense resentment. In these ways, observers can improve their skill at making helpful, insightful criticisms in highly sensitive situations. They can also gain insights about their own interpretive processes through comparing their perceptions of what they thought was significant about the scene just played, and what meanings should be attached to certain behaviors, with the perceptions of other observers.

*Conduct the Debriefing Carefully.* If the role play can be videotaped this can be enormously helpful in the debriefing and analysis session. What is particularly important is for players and observers to give their own interpretations of what has just transpired as it was seen and immediately experienced and then to compare these perceptions with what is revealed on the videotape. The discrepancies can be staggering and very informative.

I suggest a four-stage debriefing process. First, allow the actors the chance to give some account of their feelings during the role play. Let them talk about what pleased and worried them about the scene, what they feel could be improved in their own actions, and what issues they think are unresolved. Second, allow the observers to ask questions of the players about their actions and the instincts, reasoning, and assumptions that informed these. During this phase of observer questioning, the emphasis is on eliciting information. Critical comments and judgments should be kept to a minimum.

Third, ask the observers to talk about their own interpretations of the scene's events—what they regard as key actions, which behaviors they feel were helpful and which ill-advised, and what they would have wished to see happen that didn't occur. Ask them to reflect on what these interpretations tell them about their own frames of reference and structures of understanding. Observers should gain as much insight about the unquestioned assumptions and contextual judgments underlying their own perspectives as the active participants do about theirs.

Fourth, invite the observers to talk to the actors directly about what they felt were the most important elements of the scene, what they felt was most useful to their own understanding of such situations, how they would have played things differently, and so on. Some teachers make the mistake of going straight to this stage as soon as the role play has ended without establishing the more reflective, analytical atmosphere evolved during the first three stages. Role plays are not just about how well, or how badly, the actors performed in their roles. They are just as much about observers coming to a greater awareness of their own perceptual filters.

## Role Reversal

In terms of helping students become aware of their taken-for-granted assumptions—a central process of critical thinking—the variant of role play known as *role reversal* is very effective. Role reversal is commonly used in negotiation seminars, industrial training, marital therapy, and cross-cultural education. The actors involved are briefed on roles with which they come into frequent contact but have never experienced themselves. During the debriefing they talk about how it felt to be inside someone else's skin and also about their perceptions of and reactions to the actions of those playing opposite them.

This technique provides a valuable way of helping people see themselves as others see them. A student can analyze the actions of another person in the role play who is playing the role the student normally plays in real life. Role reversal is a dramatic technique, and its very drama can obscure the central purpose of the exercise, which is to aid participants' reflections on the assumptions under which they normally operate. It is not uncommon for people to become so enamored of their parts that they view the exercise as pure drama and as a chance to show off their acting ability. So role reversal should generally only be used when you feel you know your students' personalities reasonably well and when you are familiar enough with their real-life situations to gauge what would be the most useful reversals for them to experience.

## Critical Debate

A particular kind of role reversal you might wish to try is *critical debate*. In critical debate, learners are asked to explore an idea or take a position that they find unsympathetic, immoral, or distasteful. They do this as members of a debate team, rather than in a full role play. This makes the exercise more palatable to those who, for whatever reason, are so repelled by the role they are being asked to assume in a role reversal that it is impossible for them to participate.

### Critical Debate Instructions

1. Frame a controversial motion on an issue that you know inspires strongly divergent feelings and opinions in students.

2. Ask group members to volunteer to speak for or against the motion. Not surprisingly, you will find that students generally volunteer for the team closest to their own point of view.

3. Ask students to reverse their chosen preference; in other words, ask all those who volunteered to speak for the motion to speak against it, and vice versa. As you make this request, explain in detail why you're taking such a surprising, and apparently sneaky, course of action. Stress the benefits of being asked to argue against the view one habitually holds. To those who protest that this offends their own deeply held convictions, point out that the best way of defending one's

ideas against the attacks of unsympathetic critics is to have a
full understanding and appreciation of why one's critics feel
as they do. This allows one to prepare a defense that is more
likely to convince critics and helps one to anticipate the main
points of their arguments.

4. Give clear instructions about the timing of the exercise:
1 to 30 minutes: Students form into two teams—one to support the motion, and one to oppose it. Each team comes
  up with the best arguments it can to defend its case and
  nominates one or two spokespersons to present these in the
  debate.
30 to 40 minutes: Team A supports the motion.
40 to 50 minutes: Team B opposes the motion.
50 to 60 minutes: Both teams discuss among themselves their
  rebuttals of the other team's arguments.
60 to 65 minutes: Team A presents its rebuttal arguments.
65 to 70 minutes: Team B presents its rebuttal arguments.
70 to 90 minutes: Participants come out of their teams to
  discuss in a large group the experience of arguing for
  beliefs and ideas that they do not personally hold.

### The Importance of Trust

Although simulations and role plays are the most common
experiential learning methods, others are also available. There
are forms of experimental and improvisational drama that
involve audience and actors in creating and working through
scenes focusing on commonly shared dilemmas. The increased accessibility of video technology means that learning
groups can create their own film documentaries or dramas.
Teachers can use visual triggers to learning such as photogra-
phy, drawing, painting, and songwriting—all of which are
welcomed by those learners uncomfortable with teaching
approaches that rely exclusively on the written or spoken
word. Many educational programs feature internships in
which teaching sessions focus chiefly on the common analysis
of individual experience.

Crucial to the success of these experiential methods is the elusive element of trust between students and teachers. At certain specific times, the need for a high level of trust is dramatically evident—for example, when you ask students to switch the sides they had volunteered to join in the critical debate. More generally, because of the emotionally charged nature of participating in role plays and simulations, students need to feel that they are not being taken advantage of or being made to look foolish for no good educational reason.

You must always explain why you are asking students to subject themselves to the embarrassment as well as the excitement of these exercises, but your explanations will be much more readily believed if they occur against a background and history of consistent and honest actions on your part. If students don't trust you at a very basic level, then they will either hold back from participating fully in these exercises, or they will be frozen with the anxiety induced by what they see as the need to give a good performance. Building trust between teachers and students is, as Chapter Twelve demonstrates, an important affective underpinning of all meaningful education. It is never more important than with simulations and role plays.

*ᔐᒉᗌ* CHAPTER TEN

# Giving Helpful
# Evaluations

Giving evaluations is one of the most difficult, demanding, and complex tasks teachers have to face; yet, done well, it is also one of the most significant spurs to learning. Because teachers' evaluations are invested with enormous significance by students, many of whom have built up confident social faces and strong protective walls around their fragile egos, a critical comment from a teacher can be psychologically devastating. So, giving evaluations is, quite rightly, the feature of practice that gives rise to the most continuous soul-searching among many college teachers throughout their careers. And this is as it should be. If we forget for a moment the enormous significance our evaluative comments have for students and the tremendous difference such comments can make to the direction, intensity, and overall experience of their learning, then we lose much of our sensitivity as teachers. Constantly asking yourself whether your evaluative judgments are fair and helpful and whether you're avoiding the traps of favoritism and prejudice is one sign of critically responsive teaching.

Evaluations are frequently contentious judgments that reflect the political reality of education. To evaluate something is to make a value judgment about its worth. To say that one paper is better than another or that one instrumental performance is good whereas another is poor is to make judg-

132

ments on the basis of certain criteria. These criteria are usually fixed by those in positions of power—teachers, examining boards, licensing agencies, ministries of education, and
so on. They reflect the reality that students' actions and ideas
are often judged according to standards generated by figures of authority who are several stages removed from the
classroom.

Some teachers feel uncomfortable with this reality and
argue that evaluations are value-free measurements of students' performance according to objective indicators. But no
indicators are completely "objective" in the sense of being
free from human judgment. In the last analysis, all indicators
rest upon someone's belief that acting and thinking in certain
ways are better than acting and thinking in other ways. To
teach is to judge. Talking about nonjudgmental teaching,
nondirective teaching, or nonevaluative teaching is conceptually nonsensical. As Freire (Shor and Freire, 1987, p. 172)
points out:

> Education always has a directive nature we can't
> deny. The teacher has a plan, a program, a goal
> for the study. But there is the directive *liberating*
> educator on the one hand, and the directive
> *domesticating* educator on the other. The liberat-
> ing educator is different from the domesticating
> one because he or she moves more and more
> towards a moment in which an atmosphere of
> comradery is established in class. This does not
> mean that the teacher is equal to the students or
> becomes an equal to the students. No. The
> teacher begins different and ends different. The
> teacher gives grades and assigns papers to write.
> The students do not grade the teacher or give the
> teacher homework assignments! The teacher
> must also have a critical competence in his or
> her own subject that is different from the students
> and which the students should insist on. But,
> here is the central issue: In the liberating class-

room, these differences are not antagonistic ones,
as they are in the authoritarian classroom. The
liberating difference is a tension which the
teacher tries to overcome by a democratic attitude
to his or her own directiveness.

Three important points about giving evaluations are
made in this comment by Freire. The first, and most obvious,
is that teaching is inevitably value-laden. The evaluative criteria by which we decide that some educational directions are
more just, humane, or equitable than others are, at root, value
judgments. Teachers always have an agenda, a direction in
which they wish to take their students that they believe is
better than other directions. Being aware of this is at the
heart of critically responsive teaching. As Freire also says,
"For me, education is always directive, always. The question
is to know towards what and with whom it is directive" (Shor
and Freire, 1987, p. 109).

Second, Freire speaks of how liberating educators move
towards collegial, collaborative modes of education. In evaluative terms, this is seen when teachers and students evolve
evaluative criteria together, when teachers encourage self-evaluation and peer evaluation as a regular feature of their students' learning, or when the evaluative criteria established by
teachers are placed before students for their scrutiny and made
subject to some form of negotiation. Negotiating evaluative
criteria is one of the most powerfully liberating educational
activities teachers and students can experience. Doing this
cuts to the heart of the political dimensions of teaching.

Third, there is the difference Freire implies between
authoritarian and authoritative teaching. The former imposes
its will by the sheer force of tradition or institutional power.
The latter imposes its will through the credibility, trust, and
authenticity teachers establish in students' eyes. As Chapter
Twelve discusses, one of the things students value most in
teachers is credibility, the "critical competence" Freire spoke
of in his quotation. Credibility imbues students with a sense
that they are in the presence of someone whose expertise and

experience are of sufficient depth, length, and breadth that being under their direction will be valuable for their learning. Teachers who possess this credibility are authoritative teachers.

### Helpful and Unhelpful Evaluations

As a way of beginning the examination of helpful and unhelpful evaluations, let me give two examples of favorable evaluations. Both of these are imaginary but both are, I think, recognizable.

#### Favorable Evaluation 1

This paper is terrific. Well done. You've made a lot of progress since your last assignment, and you can feel well pleased with your efforts. Keep up the good work.

#### Favorable Evaluation 2

This paper is terrific. Well done. You've made a lot of progress since your last assignment, particularly in three important areas:

1. You're much more careful about citing evidence in support of your arguments, for example at the bottom of page 12 where you're proposing critical thinking as an important domain of learning and on pages 17–19 in your discussion of how education textbooks tend to ignore ethical questions.
2. You've taken much greater trouble to acknowledge viewpoints opposed to and critical of your own—see, for example, your acknowledgment of Skinner's work on page 7.
3. You're cutting down on your use of impenetrable jargon. Pages 4–6 and 11–13 were models of clear writing, though some of your old habits are still showing through, as in the discussion of Brookfield's work on page 8.

Next time you try an assignment like this, try and build on your improvements in these three areas and see if you can cut the jargon down even further. You might want to imagine that you're reading your paper to a good friend of yours who knows nothing about education. When you come across a word or phrase that you think this imaginary friend wouldn't understand, think about either deleting this, or rewriting it to make it more accessible. For example, you throw in terms like *critical reflection* (p. 8), *praxis* (p. 10) and *empowerment* (p. 3) without defining or explaining them—would your imaginary friend immediately know what these mean? But overall, you can feel well pleased with your efforts. Keep up the good work.

What are the differences (apart from length) between these two evaluations, both of which, I imagine, students would be very pleased to receive? The first is much less personalized than the second. In fact, the first evaluation comprises a number of generic comments that could, conceivably, be made about several assignments from the same batch. In contrast, students receiving the second evaluation will feel that they are respected enough by a teacher to have their work taken seriously and read carefully.

The second evaluation also clearly describes the specific aspects of the student's work that were so favorable. The first evaluation leaves a student with a warm glow, but it contains nothing from which the student can learn. The student knows that he or she has done well and for many this will be enough in and of itself. But exactly why he or she has done so well, and what it is about the work that is so meritorious, is never made clear.

The second evaluation also has a strong future-orientation. The recipient knows she has done well and takes pleasure in her achievement, but she is also directed, in clear and specific terms, to areas on which she can work the next time she tries to write another assignment like this. So, although students might be glad to receive either of these evaluations, they can only learn something useful from one of them.

Now we turn to two examples of highly critical evaluations, both of which focus on a graduate student's performance in a class on critical thinking. Again, both of these evaluations are imaginary but both, I hope, have the ring of truth about them.

### Unfavorable Evaluation 1

I need to write to you about your behavior in class a couple of weeks ago. I don't like to say this, but I'm afraid that if you carry on with your disruptive pattern of behavior I'm going to have to ask you to leave the group. You're having a really unfortunate effect on some people, and the needs of the majority must always take precedence over the individual. So try not to be so disruptive in future.

### Unfavorable Evaluation 2

I need to write to you about your behavior in class yesterday. Please accept my comments in the spirit in which they're made. In the long run, I think you'll be glad that someone cared enough to point out aspects of your behavior of which you weren't aware.

I think you could be a terrific member of this group. Your enthusiasm, drive, and experience are valuable assets to any class, and I'm glad we have them in ours. But some things are happening to obscure the value of these assets.

Let me mention three things that happened in yesterday's class that I think are worth your attention:

1. In the small-group exercise where your group was discussing the ways critical thinking was important in adult life, you spoke so much that in the fifteen minutes allowed for this exercise, I only noticed the other three group members speaking once. You are entitled to have your voice listened to seriously, but you spoke so quickly and confidently yesterday that the other group members could find no space in which to make their own, less forceful, contributions.
2. During the large-group session in which small groups gave reports on their discussion, you nominated yourself as your group's reporter and then did not acknowledge that any of the points in your report came from anyone but you.

I think your colleagues in the group would have liked some recognition.

3. When Stephanie was making her presentation, I, and the rest of the group, heard you make loud jokes about "a woman's place" and men "being on top" that distracted the group's attention and threw her off her stride.

If these kinds of behavior continue, I'm concerned that your credibility in the group will be seriously weakened. It would be a real shame if class members closed their ears to your insights just because of some unfortunate behaviors on your part of which you're probably unaware. So I'd like you to begin a self-conscious pattern of behavior change when the class meets next week. In particular, try to do the following specific things:

1. In the small-group exercise don't be the reporter who gives an account of the group's discussions to the larger class.

2. In both the large- and small-group discussions, after you have made a contribution, please wait until at least two other contributions have been made before you speak again. You can forget this rule, however, if someone asks you a question directly or wants you to explain something you've just said.

3. When you feel the impulse to crack a joke while another group member is talking, think about how you'd feel if someone made jokes during your presentation and keep your joke for the break time when you can tell it privately, and directly, to the person involved.

You may think I'm making a mountain out of a molehill, but why don't you try my suggestions for at least next week's class. Then we can meet after class to talk about what we both thought happened.

Please feel free to call me or to come and see me about this note if anything I've said is unclear to you. Next week I'll be in the office Tuesday and Wednesday afternoons and all day Thursday if you want to chat. Remember, my number is (212) 678-3701.

Both these evaluations would be hard to receive and both would, I'm sure, leave a student feeling threatened, not to say devastated. There is no way to entirely anesthetize away the pain of critical evaluations. But there are some important differences between the two examples given.

The first evaluation leaves the student overwhelmed with feelings of shame and anger, but with no sense of exactly what he or she is doing wrong. The only message received is that the student is bad and that this badness must be removed as soon as possible. But why he or she is bad, what it is that must be stopped, and how the student can change for the better are never revealed. Note also that the first evaluation is given two weeks after the event, by which time the student's memory of the class will have faded.

In contrast, the second evaluation is given immediately, which heightens its significance for the student. The evaluation points to specific actions the teacher finds distressing. It suggests in very clear and concrete terms what the student might do to improve the situation. Instead of being condemned for disruptive behavior, the student is told why it is in his or her own best interests to consider changing. Also, the student is more likely to feel respected while being criticized because the teacher deliberately and repeatedly acknowledges the student's experience and enthusiasm. The possibility of the student's reacting to the evaluation is raised by the suggestion that teacher and student meet after the next class or that the student call the teacher to talk further. There are few worse things for a student than to keep the shame, anger, and embarrassment of receiving a critical evaluation bottled up without the chance to talk through some of these feelings with their instigator.

### Characteristics of Helpful Evaluations

Several characteristics of helpful evaluations emerge from these examples and commentary.

*Clarity.* Be as clear as possible in your evaluative judgments. Let students know from the outset what criteria will be used to judge their efforts. Describe specific actions you find favorable or unfavorable and on which you want students to concentrate. Give your comments in terms and language people understand.

*Immediacy.* Give any evaluative judgments as soon as you can after the events on which you are commenting, before the pressures of life outside the classroom flood in to engage the students' attention.

*Regularity.* Try to comment regularly on students' work. Even if you only acknowledge that people are following your suggestions well, this is still important for students to hear. When you are asking for major changes to be made, you need to monitor these closely, especially in view of the learning rhythm of incremental fluctuation (two steps forward, one step back) that is so characteristic of significant learning.

*Accessibility.* Provide opportunities for further discussion and consultation regarding your evaluations. It is important for students reeling from the shock of critical comments to know that they have the chance to respond to your comments, to seek clarification, and to discuss with you any aspects of the evaluation that disturb them.

*Individualized.* Make clear that you respect the person's work enough to give detailed, clearly individualized attention to their efforts. But, when you personalize your evaluations, make sure that any criticisms you make focus on the student's actions, not on his or her personality. Don't let people feel that their whole being is under assault.

*Affirming.* Always acknowledge the students' efforts and achievements, however slight these might seem to you, before making any critical comments about their work. Very rarely, I would suggest, will you come across work that is without any redeeming features whatsoever. Show that you're acknowledging what is good (even if this is only to take account of the effort someone has put into a piece) at the same time that you draw attention to what needs work.

*Future-Oriented.* Give clear suggestions about what specific actions students should take in the short and long run.

*Justifiable.* Be careful to describe how attending to your criticisms is in the students' best interests. People have a right to know why you're criticizing them. They need to be sure that they spring from your concern for their learning, not from your own obsessions.

*Educative.* Keep asking yourself, "What can this person learn from my comments?" A good evaluation is one from which students can learn. Evaluations should not leave students just feeling good or bad about what they've done; they should provide guidance as well. If students only feel warmed or ashamed by your evaluation then it isn't educative.

### Improving Your Evaluations

Compared to the reams of advice available in textbooks concerning how to improve your teaching, there is relatively little attention given to improving your evaluations. When the process of evaluation is examined, the focus tends to be either on evaluating teaching effectiveness or on evaluating broad program outcomes. The following section describes how, as a teacher, you can give evaluations that display the characteristics outlined in the previous section.

*Experience Being Evaluated.* One of the first things you can do is to place yourself in the position of being a learner whose efforts are being evaluated. One of the most profound professional development efforts you can undertake is to experience learning something difficult and then to reflect on the significance and implications of this for your teaching. This is never more dramatically true than with evaluation. If those who regularly give evaluations of others' efforts have their own efforts subjected to regular evaluation, they are much more likely to be sensitive to the aspects of evaluation that assist and affirm, rather than those that merely demean.

For example, as someone who is himself a writer, but who also regularly evaluates students' writings, it is crucial for me to reflect on how I respond when my own work is criticized. In draft form my manuscripts (particularly my book manuscripts) are often criticized for their obscure language, their lack of practicality, their tendency to repetition, and their political tone. When I first receive these criticisms I always react emotionally to them. My first impulse is to get straight on the phone to the editors concerned and to harangue them for their lack of judgment in choosing such obviously uninformed reviewers to comment on my work. Even though, rationally, I know I am being unfair and reacting instinctively and defensively, I still feel it as strongly each time the reviews of my work in draft come to me.

Gradually, however, I settle down and give the reviews a second, third, and fourth reading, and it is then that I start to make some judgments about these evaluations of my work. If a review of my draft manuscript is wholly negative, it loses credibility in my eyes, since I cannot believe that something I have poured my heart and intellect into over many months or years can be entirely without merit. Of course, it may objectively be the case that my work is without merit. But saying this alone leaves me with no sense of self-respect. So, as a way of protecting my self-esteem, I reject the evaluation out of hand.

If, however, a reviewer acknowledges what is good about the draft, as well as what is bad, then I immediately give that person's negative comments much greater credibility. I also pay careful attention to any suggestions this reviewer makes, since I have some trust in his or her evenhandedness. On the other hand, generalized, blanket criticisms that cast doubt on the whole of my work yet give me no examples of my errors are of little use. Without the chance to see these errors, I have no chance to make any assessment of the accuracy of these criticisms. So a review that says, for example,

"This manuscript is ponderously written and has little connection to the practical realities of classroom life," but which gives no specific illustrations of these faults serves only to frustrate me. I can't learn anything from it.

Now if I, as someone who has written books and articles and won prizes for some of these, feel this way when I receive evaluations of my own work, how much more intensely are students going to feel the devastation of having their works criticized by me in these ways? Knowing how dispiriting receiving poor evaluations can be and knowing how frustrating generalized criticisms can be makes me much more sensitive to the effects my own evaluations have on students. I always try to be affirmative and respectful, to focus on specifics, to suggest things that can be worked on, and to give students the chance to react to my criticisms by seeking further clarification of any ambiguities.

So if you haven't had the chance to learn anything difficult recently, either in your own area or in one with which you are completely unfamiliar, try to take the time to experience how it feels to do this. As you have your efforts scrutinized, think about the kinds of critical comments and evaluations that make you feel respected and from which you learn something. Focus on the comments and actions that leave you feeling angry, confused, and ashamed. From these reflections, you should have some ideas about how the insights you've realized about the experience of being evaluated can be integrated into your own practice.

*Open Your Evaluative Criteria to Negotiation.* As I pointed out at the beginning of this chapter, evaluation has a strong political component. One of the most powerful things you can do as a teacher is to negotiate the evaluative criteria with the students who are being scrutinized. Sometimes negotiation can take place from scratch. More usually, however, external constraints such as institutional cultures or the demands of accrediting bodies mean that some things have to be more or less accepted, whereas others are open to compromise. For students, the experience of being involved in setting or negotiating evaluative criteria is one that makes them feel respected and attended to. For teachers, there is the strong likelihood that subjecting their evaluative criteria to students' scrutiny will result in the establishment of criteria that will mean something to learners as well as to teachers, that students will find accessible, and that, as a consequence, they will take seriously.

Of course, as Chapter Two illustrates, negotiation does not mean constant and complete agreement. Negotiation is not the same as capitulation. You should not feel obliged to agree to every request students' make. There may be some things about which, as a teacher, you feel you cannot make concessions. But even if this is the case, there is the possibility that students will suggest indicators of accomplishment and forms of evaluating their efforts that had never occurred to you.

For example, I believe that developing critical thinking is the fundamental purpose of all my efforts as a teacher. This is not something I can compromise on, and I make this clear to students at the outset of their involvement with me. But how critical thinking can be recognized, what forms it might take, and what might be the best ways of judging how someone is acquiring this skill are matters on which students have their own ideas and suggestions. They are likely, if invited, to propose indicators of critical thinking that are grounded in their own experiences and that may be, therefore, much more accessible and meaningful to them than anything I might have devised.

*Ask Your Students to Evaluate Your Evaluations.* Ask students to tell you which of your evaluative comments are most useful to them and why. This can be done individually through private conversations, or in groups through discussion. Make sure that you plan some formative evaluation sessions at regular intervals during your teaching activities. Be as open as you can to students' perceptions of the valuable aspects of their learning and to what they judge to be the most significant, emerging outcomes of the course. Encourage them to talk about what they've gained from the experience and don't worry if what they regard as the most valuable aspects of their involvement with you are not what you had planned.

As Chapter Four showed, students often remember as the most significant outcomes of educational participation insights, skills, and knowledge that were of a relatively low priority to those planning and teaching a course or workshop. As students suggest to you ways of improving a course, and in particular of giving them more helpful evaluations, show that you are listening carefully and taking them seriously. Be prepared to change your usual ways of working if their suggestions make sense, as long as you are sure that your convictions and visions aren't compromised in the process. Be ready to explain more clearly why you have arranged things as they are if you feel you can't compromise in any way.

*Promote Self-Evaluation and Peer Evaluation.* Ever since being asked to evaluate my own work when I was a graduate student, I have tried to ask the same of my own students. More than this, I have encouraged them to comment on the work of their colleagues and to submit their own efforts to colleagues for peer evaluation. In the student learning contracts that I and my colleagues supervise at Teachers College, students receive three evaluations of their work—one from a professor, one from themselves, and one from a peer. They are expected to reciprocate their receipt of evaluations from their peers by being ready to give their own evaluations of the efforts of their fellow students.

I teach a semester-long course on qualitative research methods using a variant of peer evaluation; in between each class students conduct, individually, a small research project such as designing an interview schedule, administering a critical incident, or analyzing some data given to all students the week before. When students meet each week in class, they each distribute multiple copies of their own efforts to other students. Hence, if the week's research assignment was to develop an interview schedule for the topic "How college teachers respond to students who resist learning,'' then each student gives a copy of his or her own schedule to each class member and receives, in return, a copy of each of the other students' schedules. Class time is then devoted to sifting through the assembled schedules and extracting those questions that are, by common agreement, the most penetrating and accessibly phrased. This sifting process is, in fact, an extended exercise in peer evaluation.

Helping students acquire the critically alert cast of mind that turns easily and regularly to peer and self-evaluation is a fundamental purpose of college teaching. If you instill this habit in your students, you have given them something of lasting significance. Sooner or later students leave the intellectual enclave of higher education and return to the workaday world. For them to have acquired the habit of examining their own work critically as a detached observer is an incalculable benefit.

Higher education is, or should be, a training for self-evaluation. Adopting an attitude of self-evaluation to learning is something that students can apply in all the future contexts and activities in which they are engaged. It is much more important than any content they could assimilate. Likewise, for students to have learned something of the art of peer evaluation—of giving helpful critical insights to colleagues and intimates in a manner that affirms rather than shames—develops in them in a capacity that will be sought out by their peers for years to come.

# CHAPTER ELEVEN

# Overcoming Resistance to Learning

Why people resist learning is a puzzlingly complex question, made the more so by some students who do quite well for a time and then suddenly seem to stubbornly resist doing what, to you as a teacher, seem like fairly simple operations. Nevertheless, some typical causes can be identified and some approaches can be suggested in response to make this problem seem less intractable. Even if you are at a loss to know how to deal with resistance, being aware of some of its causes (and realizing that your own actions may not be one of these) can help to decrease the demoralizing frustration you will probably feel when it is encountered.

Essentially, as most people realize, learning involves change. Since change is threatening, many people prefer to remain in situations that to outsiders seem wholly unsatisfactory, rather than to endure the psychological disruption represented by taking some kind of action. In all contexts of life we can see people for whom the threat of learning new behaviors or ideas is so unsettling that they remain in situations which will, in the long term, do them great harm. In marriages, people will put up with sustained psychological and physical assault rather than risk abandoning what is, at least, familiar. In the workplace, stagnant and oppressive organizational conditions persist simply because of the unquestioning acceptance of traditional organizational norms—of the attitude of "that's how it's done around here." Politically, repressive regimes fear (quite correctly) that allowing the free debate of ideas critical to dominant ideologies will cause people to learn ways of thinking and acting that threaten the position of those in power.

As teachers, if we remember that learning represents change and that change is perceived by many people as highly threatening, then we have taken the first step towards understanding some of the causes of resistance to learning. As always, it is useful if we can draw upon our experiences as learners to think about those times we resisted learning something new, why this was so, and what helped us overcome this reluctance. For example, as I began working on this book, I also, at the age of forty, learned to drive. Despite the inconvenience my not being a driver caused me, I preferred to engage in intricate and increasingly desperate convolutions to avoid having to face this act of learning. Things mechanical have always seemed threatening to me, and the prospect of learning to control what I regarded as a sophisticated instrument of death as much as a means of transportation was so intimidating that I resisted this sneakily and determinedly.

Seeing almost everyone I knew doing this effortlessly did not, as one might imagine, ease my anxiety; rather, it increased it, since I was convinced that if I tried to learn, I would be revealed in all my shame and embarrassment as the one person in the world who showed a total inability to drive. Eventually, a combination of circumstances encouraged me to learn this skill. My wife had often said how much it would help her if, on some of our longer drives across the Midwest, I could take the wheel for an hour or so at regular intervals. I sympathized with this, safe in the knowledge that she would not insist that I learn to drive in the madness of Manhattan, where we live. Also, since we don't own a car in New York and rely almost wholly on public transportation, there was little opportunity to learn, even if my motivation had been stronger.

After being granted tenure at Columbia, I took the customary sabbatical, and the chance to learn to drive arose. For several months of this sabbatical, we lived in a small hamlet in southern France, where most of this book was written. This environment provided ideal conditions for learning to drive. First, I could do this free from the risk of embarrassment at my failure, since friends and colleagues were three thousand miles away across the Atlantic. Second, the roads where we lived (a rural area two to three hours drive east of Avignon) were very quiet. There was little chance of any really heavy traffic. So I was in a situation where it would be hard not to succeed. Third, the expectation created for me was that I would learn to become comfortable handling the car and maneuvering on quiet country roads, no more. So realistic, achievable limits were set on what I was to try. Fourth, we leased an automatic model, so that the main impediment to driving over which I had previously always stumbled—changing gears—was removed. All I had to do was press on the accelerator and point the machine—just as I did in bumper cars as a child! Fifth, I had a teacher (my wife) who was clear, calm, and very supportive. She didn't push too fast, and she broke the activity into small, incremental chunks, gave clear instructions, praised frequently those things that were done well, and readily admitted that when she learned to drive she had the same fears and anxieties I was experiencing.

Reflecting on my experience of resisting learning and of what helped me overcome this has helped me to be more understanding of and sensitive to my own students' resistance to learning things (such as becoming critically reflective about their practice as educators) that are difficult and threatening. As you encounter resistance to your teaching, you might want to try to analyze some of your own episodes of resisting learning as a way of understanding your students' situation.

## Understanding Resistance to Learning

The following are some of the chief reasons why people resist learning. When you encounter resistance in your classes, or with individual students, you might want to ask yourself how much this is due to combinations of some of these factors.

*Poor Self-Image as Learners.* Many college students, especially those returning to college as adults, have educational histories comprised in part of systematic humiliation. They will have passed through classes in which they were told, directly or indirectly, that they were too dumb to learn. They may have picked up the impression that teachers felt they should leave education as soon as possible to leave space for those who showed an aptitude for learning.

Developing a self-image as a learner—regarding oneself as somebody who is able to acquire new skills, knowledge, and insights—is a crucial psychological underpinning to learning. It functions as a self-fulfilling prophecy. If people see themselves as learners, if this is one way in which they define their being, then the prospect of new learning is not as traumatic for them.

*Fear of the Unknown.* Perhaps the single greatest cause of resistance to learning is fear of the unknown. The change required by learning something new is profoundly unsettling for many people who much prefer to cling to the stabilities of their existence. Routine, habit, and familiarity are strongly appealing as leitmotifs for many people's personal, professional, and political lives. For some, the conduct of life is a quest for certainty, for a system of beliefs and a set of values— even for a well-defined social structure—that they can adopt, and commit to, for life.

The psychological comfort and reassurance derived from commitment to such eternal verities is so strong that it can resist years of discrepancies, dissonances, and anomalies. As people witness events that seem to contradict their beliefs and values, they often seem to become even more committed to them. It is as if a perverse psychological law sometimes seems to apply in which the strength of commitment to beliefs and values is inversely correlated with the amount of evidence encountered that contradicts the truth of these. The human capacity for denial knows no limits. Even for students who willingly embrace the change endemic to learning, there is often a sense of trepidation about the future and a grieving for lost certainties.

*A Normal Rhythm of Learning.* Some instances of resistance to learning are simply examples of the incremental fluctuation identified in Chapter Four as a typical rhythm of significant learning. As people learn something new, they often find that their initial embracing of new ideas, attitudes, or practices is followed by a yearning to return to the comfortable certainties of yesterday. This form of resistance is temporary; it is the second part of the "two steps forward, one step back" rhythm. But, although temporary, it is experienced just as deeply as other forms of resistance.

*Lack of Clarity in Teachers' Instructions.* If learning is suffused with ambiguity, if students are unsure what is expected of them and by what criteria their efforts are being judged, they will probably mistrust teachers and resist their instructions and entreaties. In critical incident reports, the perception of ambiguity—of being unsure what teachers want or expect and of suspecting that they hold secret agendas—is reported time and again as one of the most demoralizing factors for students.

*Students' Personal Dislike of Teachers.* Since learning is such an emotionally experienced phenomenon, a student's dislike of a teacher as a person can become so overwhelming that it interferes with all their interactions. Teachers' personalities are inevitably reflected in their educational actions. They may use humor inappropriately; make racist or sexist remarks; dismay some by their informality and offend others by their unapproachability; exhibit favoritism and discrimination; and appear arrogant, cynical, naive, or uncaring—all quite without realizing that this is happening.

*Disjunction of Learning and Teaching Styles.* Sometimes it is not the content that students resist but the style in which teachers teach and in which they, as students, are asked to learn. Students who have been used to learning primarily through listening to lectures and reading independently will probably be confused and intimidated at the sudden prospect of participating in a role play. People who are irritated with group process, who see discussions as a waste of time and a distraction from the really important activities associated with independent study, will probably resist case studies, simulations, and debates. Teachers who rely on only one teaching method must always expect a hard core of resisters who are unsympathetic to or intimidated by the approach concerned.

*Apparent Irrelevance of the Learning Activity.* If the learning activities people are asked to undertake seem to have no connection to or meaning for their own interests and concerns, they may well resist them. College study, particularly for students who are returning after a period out in the work force, frequently demands a heavy price. If someone has dipped deep into their financial reserves, resigned from a secure job, undergone all kinds of convolutions to arrange child care or work coverage while they are learning, and faced resistance from unsympathetic spouses, friends, or colleagues, then they are going to be frustrated and annoyed if they think that they are being asked to perform exercises or undertake assignments that have no meaning for them.

*Fear of Looking Foolish in Public.* Many people (myself included) only want to do things that they know they can do well. They will only play games they know they can win, and they will only try something new and difficult if this can be done in private. Students' egos are fragile creations and, as the discussion of the impostor syndrome in Chapter Four showed, this fragility is as characteristic of those who appear confident and successful as it is of those whose experience of life has been oppressive. So students' resistance to a particular learning activity may simply reflect their feeling that it is occurring in an overly public forum rather than their dislike for the focus of the learning itself.

*Danger of Committing Cultural Suicide.* Participating in education is a highly valued activity in some subcultures, but in others it is extremely threatening. A student's decision to attend college may entail many social and psychological changes. One of these is the risk of students' being regarded with suspicion or mistrust in their home cultures and of eventually being excluded from these. These cultures may tolerate participation in education if it is felt that students will thereby be better equipped to promote the culture's values and activities. But if students are asked to contemplate too much that is new or to change in ways the culture sees as too radical, then they will be given the message that further participation calls into question their allegiance to the culture and will be dealt with summarily.

Faced with the psychologically devastating prospect of losing their cultural identities and supports, many students, not surprisingly, choose not to pay the price required by learning. I have seen this form of cultural control exercised by working-class cultures in which taking education seriously (that is, accepting the innate appeal of intellectual inquiry rather than viewing it solely as a means of making money) is seen by some as a betrayal of solid, unpretentious, working-class values. I have seen it exercised by religious fundamentalists for whom a member's consenting exposure to new ideas is evidence of blasphemy. I have also seen it in ethnic groups where participation in education past a certain culturally allowed point is taken to mean that learners have either joined the alien host culture or are insulting the values learned in childhood. So some resistance to learning may be the result of students sensing that if they go past a certain point they will be committing cultural suicide.

*Level of Required Learning is Inappropriate.* A teacher can easily misinterpret students' levels of learning readiness. Resistance to learning can arise if the tasks teachers require of students are pitched at too abstract or conceptually sophisticated a level. For teachers who are caught up in the passion of communicating the beauty of scientific reasoning, literary insight, or historical theories, it is easy to overestimate how far students have progressed. If teachers travel too fast and too far for students, and if they never check behind to see that students are keeping up with their pace, then they run a real risk of leaving them far behind. If this happens, and if students are asked to undertake tasks that are far too complex for them, it is not surprising if they respond with resistance.

## Overcoming Resistance to Learning

In this section I propose a number of responses you might consider when you encounter sustained and deeply felt resistance to learning. Before discussing these, however, let me make the general point that the intensity and amount of resistance you encounter will probably be reduced considerably if you pay attention to some of the general principles of teaching outlined throughout this book. So if you make a deliberate attempt to create diversity in your teaching, to explore students' experience of learning, to balance challenge and support, and to see yourself, primarily, as a helper of learning rather than a classroom performer, then you are already teaching in a way that responds effectively to resistance.

*Ask Yourself Whether the Resistance Is Justified.* Don't immediately assume that because someone resists a learning activity they are being obtuse. Don't immediately think that all you need to do is to be a bit more skillful in justifying your actions or in designing the exercises. Try to make sure that the learning they're resisting is really in their own best interests and not being required simply because of institutional routine or because of your own private obsessions. Having asked yourself these awkward questions and having decided that the learning is something you feel is important for students to experience (even though they disagree), you will be in a much stronger psychological position to argue your case and to weather students' resistance. And if, after having answered these questions honestly, you decide that your insistence on this learning isn't really justified, then you'll have saved yourself a lot of time, energy, and heartache.

***Try to Sort Out the Causes of the Resistance.*** Since resistance is such a complex phenomenon, an important first step is for you to gain some sense of which combination of factors is causing resistance in a student or group of students. Before thinking about responses, you must have a clear idea of the causes, for otherwise you run the real risk of spending large amounts of time pursuing irrelevant solutions. Try to speak to resisters individually; ask class members to complete critical incidents on the highs and lows of classroom life; read their learning journals; and regularly invite criticism, interpretation, and evaluation of the educational processes they are experiencing. The nature and causes of the resistance you encounter will affect the responses you feel are appropriate.

***Research Your Students' Backgrounds and Cultures.*** Find out about your students' backgrounds and histories—their values, expectations, cultural allegiances, and preferred learning styles. This will help you to avoid teaching in ways that confirm students' poor self-images. You will be less likely to rely on methods and approaches that are wholly unfamiliar to them or to use materials they find offensive or incomprehensible. You will be better placed to demonstrate for students the meaning and connectedness of the learning activities you are asking them to undertake. And you will be more aware of those lines that students feel they can't cross for fear of committing cultural suicide.

***Involve Students in Educational Planning.*** Whenever you can, involve students in planning the general focus, specific content, educational methods, and evaluative procedures of the learning activity. The extent to which this is possible varies according to context, and sometimes external factors will mean that almost all of these features will have been prescribed beforehand. But if it can be done, involving students has several benefits: It removes some of their fear of the unknown, makes students feel respected and valued, and increases the likelihood of your teaching having some meaning for them. All these factors help to reduce the learner resistance that might otherwise have arisen.

*Conduct Regular Formative Evaluation Sessions.* Take the time, deliberately and explicitly, to ask students what problems they see arising, what aspects of teaching they find ambiguous, and how, unwittingly, you might be arousing resistance. For example, I begin every one of my classes with an open-ended troubleshooting session in which I invite students to raise issues, make complaints, and ask questions. I anticipate spending 20 to 25 percent of the total class time on this, since I feel it is so important. Sometimes, of course, there is little to say and we can proceed with the class after a couple of minutes. But, despite the impatience exhibited by some students at what they clearly feel is an unproductive waste of time, an enormous amount of information has emerged from these sessions to make my teaching more critically responsive. Through giving students the chance to air their fears and express their confusion, you will be more likely to anticipate serious resistance.

*Explain Your Intentions Clearly.* Explain as clearly as you can why you are asking students to develop certain skills, explore areas of knowledge, and participate in exercises you have devised. If you use standardized evaluation forms, distribute these along with the instructions for the assignment so that students can see exactly how their efforts will be judged. Never assume that students consent to or approve of your actions. Because of the authority you have in students' eyes, it will often be difficult for them to challenge you directly about your intentions. So be ready to make these clear at the outset. Having a clearly developed critical rationale for practice as advocated in Chapter Two will help you explain and justify your intentions convincingly.

*Justify Why You Think Learning Is Important.* Some teachers are so personally convinced of the innate validity of their activities that they forget that these need to be justified to students. Don't be too proud to say why you are convinced that it's important for people to learn something. Be ready to describe the benefits you believe learning brings in terms that contribute to students' well-being, insight, and capacity for survival rather than in terms that relate to your own concerns. Take students to situations outside the classroom where the benefits of the learning activity are clearly in evidence. Don't feel (as some do) that demonstrating the importance of learning smacks of grubby intellectual salesmanship.

*Involve Former Resisters.* In trying to convince students of the importance of a learning activity, you are always working against the fact that your own expressions of its importance will be met with some degree of skepticism. Students will say, "Of course you're going to tell us it's important that we learn this; it's in your own interest to say so—after all, that's how you earn your living." But the voices that will have far greater credibility than yours are those of former students who were themselves resistant to learning but who came to appreciate its value for them. Inviting to class former students who were initially skeptical of learning something, but who found that doing this came to be extremely important in their lives, is a very effective way of reducing resistance. A few words from these former students will have a much greater effect than any number of appeals you can make. So whenever people who were resistant to a learning activity contact you to tell you how much it helped them and how much it meant for them at a later time, take down their phone numbers and ask them if they would mind visiting your class sometime to say this to your current group of students.

*Create Situations in Which Students Succeed.* Think how you can break down learning activities into specific tasks and incremental chunks. When you have done this, try to find for each task or chunk at least one activity or requirement that even the most anxiety-ridden of your students can perform to some minimum standard of success. The activity need not be profound or be regarded by you as of particular significance. Put your judgments about this aside and reflect on how important it will be for students who are paralyzed with fear or frozen with anxiety to be able to experience some form of success, however small. Nothing is more heartening or enhancing to learning than feeling that one is moving forward successfully. Creating regular exercises in which it is very hard for students not to succeed will go a long way toward molding their self-images as effective learners.

*Accentuate the Positive.* Whenever possible, acknowledge students' efforts, congratulate them on their progress, and stress what is good in their performance. Remember that what may seem like a very small incremental move forward to you may be a progression of enormous significance to the person involved. By building their self-confidence and developing in them a sense that they are making progress and moving forward, you will help lessen their fear of the unknown. Make sure that you precede all critical comments—both written and spoken—with some acknowledgment of other aspects of their efforts.

*Encourage Peer Learning and Peer Teaching.* Since many students find it intimidating to be required to perform in front of a teacher whom they perceive as a person of enormous expertise and authority, try and create some opportunities for more private learning through peer tutoring (Topping, 1988; Goodlad and Hirst, 1989). As we know, the support of a learning community of peers can make a crucial difference to whether or not people persist in learning. Parrainage and learning partnerships are increasingly recognized as important alternatives to more common forms of small-group work. Many colleges have instituted buddy systems, whereby new students are paired with students who have been in a program for some time. The more experienced students guide the newer ones through the first traumatic stages of the program, offering advice, materials, and support. Asking students to work in pairs or triads, suggesting that learners take turns in evaluating each other's efforts, and asking more experienced students to teach neophytes are all ways in which students' learning activities can be granted what to them is a welcome degree of privacy. Relieved from the stress of having their efforts scrutinized by the teacher, they may find that much of their resistance to learning has disappeared.

*Don't Push Too Fast.* Be realistic about what you can expect from people. Remember those times when you, as a learner, seemed stuck on a learning plateau that you thought you would never leave. Learning is such a complicated process, involving all kinds of fluctuations, rhythms, plateaus, and threats to our identities that teachers need to realize that they are in for the long haul. Sometimes students appear to resist activities that teachers see as flowing naturally from what has just been achieved. To students, however, arriving where they have arrived may have taken such energy and determination that there may be a real need for an interlude before traveling further. They may need time to work through the grieving process when old ways of thinking and doing are lost. They may need to return temporarily to familiar intellectual territory to develop the courage for the next learning effort. They may want more time than you are allowing for the reflective speculation and interpretation they find so important. They may simply be exhausted.

*Attend to the Need to Build Trust.* Because gaining people's trust is such an important part of learning, make sure that you are fair and honest. If practicable, show students that you are an advocate for them in dealing with other authority figures in the institution. Look for administrative and bureaucratic practices that are oppressive and that are needlessly creating resistance. Examine your own teaching behaviors for aspects that are oppressive, despite your own best intentions and your commitments to democratic classrooms. Be prepared to listen to criticisms of your actions, no matter how difficult they are for you to hear. In fact, the more difficult it is for you to hear criticism, the more students will respect the emotional effort you make to do this. Make sure you avoid playing favorites. Above all else, make sure that your words and actions are congruent. Don't make promises you can't keep. Don't make commitments you can't fulfill. Better to make no promises or commitments at all than to damage your credibility by not meeting them.

*Admit the Normality of Resistance.* Talk to students about your own episodes of resisting learning and the times when you shied away from the unknown for fear of looking foolish in front of your peers. Give examples of former resisters you encountered and talk about the reasons these students felt the ways they did. You may strike a chord within some people and embolden them to speak publicly about why they feel so uncertain. Acknowledging that resistance exists and admitting to its normality might seem like an embarrassing thing for teachers to do. In the long run, however, it will make everybody feel much more relaxed if the situation is made public. Far better to do this than to expect, in effect, a massive suspension of belief by pretending that everything is fine when you feel that you're facing serious and sustained resistance.

*Be Wary of Confrontational Obsession.* It is easy to become obsessed with transforming someone's resistance to learning into enthusiasm. Converting someone to seeing why, in your view, they should learn something can easily become distorted into a self-imposed test of your professional competence. Some people will remain stubbornly resistant to learning no matter what you do and no matter how much time you spend trying to convince them. At some point you need to recognize this and cut your losses. There is no point in having your energies drained by your determination to force one person to learn if this means the learning needs of the rest of your students are neglected. So don't endanger your self-respect and your morale by mistakenly interpreting your conversion of a resister as the ultimate test of your professional ability.

*Strike a Bargain with Total Resisters.* If a hard core of resisters remain for whom all your efforts and overtures mean nothing, then I would advise you to accept the situation. There are some things you can't do much about. When you get to this point, you might want to try striking a bargain with these resisters whereby you accept their right not to learn and they agree not to disrupt the learning of others. In such situations, I will sometimes have a private talk with the resister:

> Look, I know you think this is a waste of time, and I know that no matter what I say you're not going to participate in good spirit in any activities we undertake. I could try and force you to learn but that, ultimately, would mean that I didn't respect your right to decide whether or what you will learn. So let's strike a bargain. I won't push you to go through what everyone else is going through. You can choose which exercises you want to be involved in and which you want to sit out. In return, I ask you to refrain from disrupting these exercises and preventing those who are interested in participating from trying them. I won't make you learn, and you won't stop others learning.

Such an offer usually surprises students. To me, however, it has several appealing features. It acknowledges and respects students' right not to learn. It prevents me from wasting any more time trying to convince total resisters to do what I ask. It keeps students in touch with the learning activity, albeit as observers. And there is always the chance that once the pressure is removed and they are allowed to act just as observers these students will find themselves becoming interested in the activities taking place.

*Acknowledge Students' Right to Resist.* Ultimately, it is a mistake to try and force people to learn. This does not mean that you should not explain, with all the force and conviction you can muster, why you think it's in the students' own best interests to learn something. But if all your reasoning means nothing, then you must grant people the right not to learn. To some teachers who work in particularly authoritarian settings, allowing someone the right to not learn is not an option. In a repressive organizational or political regime, your life and livelihood may be in danger if you refuse to force someone to learn. But doing this destroys completely the trust between students and teachers that is so essential to significant learning. The activity becomes indoctrination, not education.

# CHAPTER TWELVE

# Building Trust
# with Students

Underlying all significant learning is the element of trust. Trust between teachers and students is the affective glue binding educational relationships together. Not trusting teachers has several consequences for students. They are unwilling to submit themselves to the perilous uncertainties of new learning. They avoid risk. They keep their most deeply felt concerns private. They view with cynical reserve the exhortations and instructions of teachers. The more profound and meaningful the learning is to students, the more they need to be able to trust their teachers.

The importance of trust is highlighted time and again in students' critical incident responses and in the studies of the experience of learning mentioned in Chapter Three. In speaking of transformative learning events, students often make explicit mention of how teachers' actions, and the trust these inspire or destroy, are crucial to learning. At the center of the cluster of characteristics that make teachers more trustworthy in students' eyes are two components that might be described as teacher credibility and teacher authenticity. These are connected but, as we shall see, they are not necessarily complementary.

## Teacher Credibility

Teacher credibility refers to teachers' ability to present themselves as people with something to offer students. When

teachers have this credibility, students see them as possessing
a breadth of knowledge, depth of insight, and length of experience that far exceeds the students' own. Freire (Shor and
Freire, 1987, p. 172) describes credibility as the "critical competence" that students have a right to expect of their teachers.
Students continually stress their desire to be in the presence
of someone whose knowledge, skill, and expertise mean that
they can help students come to grips with some of the contradictions, complexities, and dilemmas they are experiencing.
Although teacher education programs often stress process
skills above content mastery, students still attach great importance to teachers' having subject and skill expertise; without
intellectual and experiential credibility, process skill is ultimately empty.

## Teacher Authenticity

Authentic teachers (Moustakas, 1966) are, essentially, those
that students feel they can trust. They are also those whom
students see as real flesh-and-blood human beings with passions, frailties, and emotions. They are remembered as whole
persons, not as people who hide behind a collection of
learned role behaviors appropriate to college teaching. In
more specific terms, students see four behaviors as evidence of
authenticity: (1) teachers' words and actions are congruent;
(2) teachers admit to error, acknowledge fallibility, and make
mistakes in full public view of learners; (3) teachers allow
aspects of their personhood outside their role as teachers to be
revealed to students; and (4) teachers respect learners by listening carefully to students' expressions of concern, by taking
care to create opportunities for students' voices to be heard,
and by being open to changing their practice as a result of
students' suggestions.

## Taking Steps to Build Trust

Trust is not given to teachers as a right, and teachers cannot
assume that it exists a priori. It must be earned. In particular,

the teachers' right to challenge students is not a given. Only if teachers have first displayed a public willingness to be learners themselves by adopting a critical stance towards their own actions and ideas can they legitimately ask for the same critical stance to be demonstrated by their students.

You must remember that not only can you not expect students to trust you from the outset, you may also have to face accumulations of mistrust nurtured by the actions of cynical and arrogant teachers in the past. When you face students for the first time, you also face their accumulated educational histories and their memories of all the teachers they have experienced in the past.

Building trust is neither quick nor easy. It can be very dispiriting to realize that your efforts to build trust may often bring little immediate result. But remember that, in Carl Rogers's words (1980, p. 273) "students have been 'conned' for so long that a teacher who is real with them is usually seen for a time as simply exhibiting a new brand of phoniness." With persistance, however, and with attention to some of the factors and processes described in this chapter, it is possible to build trust where none has existed before. If you do this, students will remember the time they spent with you as a time when they were valued and affirmed.

*Don't Deny Your Credibility.* One of the most erroneous and damaging beliefs held by some college teachers concerns the best way to show that they value students' experiences. There is a tendency among these teachers to try to dignify the validity of students' experiences by belittling their own. This is a serious mistake. Teachers may believe that if they say to students, "Look, my own experiences have no greater innate validity than yours—you'll teach me as much as I teach you," they are recognizing and affirming students' life experiences. In fact, the reverse can be true.

Teachers' protestations that they don't really know any more than students do and that they are simply there to help students realize that they already possess the knowledge and skills they need sound supportive and respectful. But such

protestations from teachers who are demonstrably more skillful, more intellectually able, and possessed of a much greater
range of experience than that of students will be perceived as
false. Instead of students warming to what teachers believe to
be admirably humane and respectful attitudes, students may
conclude that if teachers' experiences have left them with no
greater skill, knowledge, or insight than that possessed by
students, then there is nothing useful students can learn from
them. So in your desire to affirm the validity of your students'
experiences and abilities, be careful not to undermine your
own credibility in their eyes.

***Be Explicit About Your Organizing Vision.*** In Chapter Two I
argued that teachers cannot avoid having visions that guide
their practice. This is quite normal. What is problematic for
students, however, is when teachers deny having any visions,
yet through their actions make it apparent that such visions
exist and are highly influential in determining what happens
in the classroom.

     I have an educational agenda, and I always try to
acknowledge this fact plainly to students. Instead of pretending that I have no power in the classroom, that anything
goes as far as curricula, methods, or evaluative criteria are
concerned, I try to make explicit at the outset what my expectations and organizing principles are. In interviews with appli-
cants for degree programs, in consultations with students who
are interested in finding out about my courses, and in all the
course descriptions I circulate, I state the evaluative criteria
that inform my teaching.

     On the first meeting of any new course, I advise stu-
dents to regard their attendance as a provisional sampling, a
testing of the water. If they object to my agenda and concerns,
then they can leave after this first meeting with no ill feeling.
I will make sure that I say something like the following at
this meeting:

          If you decide to join this class, you must expect
          to be asked to be critically reflective about your

own practice as educators. You must also anticipate being asked to analyze critically the con-
gruences and discrepancies between your experiences and the pronouncements of theorists and
researchers who are regarded as experts. These
features are nonnegotiable, and you should know
this right from the beginning. If you don't like
them, or if you feel you're not ready to do these
things, then you should think seriously about not
coming to the second meeting of class. If you do
show up next week, then I'll take this as indicating that you accept these fundamental purposes.
If you don't show up that's fine—you'll have
saved yourself a lot of needless anxiety. I know
that critically reflective education is hard to
understand and anticipate until you find yourself
immersed in it, so let's take some time now to
discuss some of the queries and uncertainties that
I'm sure you have about what staying in this
class involves.

Having said this I can then negotiate in good faith
with students about possible changes in methods, areas of
content, and evaluative indicators by which the development
of critical reflection can be recognized. Not to make explicit
right at the outset the fact that I have an organizing vision
and not to inform students of the form that vision takes in
the class would be fundamentally dishonest.

*Make Sure Your Words and Actions Are Congruent.* The con-
gruence of words and actions is absolutely paramount. Few
things destroy students' trust in teachers more quickly than
teachers who say they will do one thing and then proceed to
do something quite different or teachers who espouse one set
of philosophical aims and guiding principles and then proceed to practice in ways that render these null and void. One
of the most frequently described examples of dissonance
between teachers' words and actions concerns those teachers

who claim they are fully committed to democratic principles. Such teachers will declare that the classroom is a collaborative learning laboratory in which students will have a full and equal role in determining what happens. Yet, subtly and manipulatively, teachers override students' concerns and expressed wishes to do what they, as teachers, feel is important.

Such spuriously democratic teachers will tell students at the outset of a class that the curriculum, methods, and evaluative criteria are in students' hands. As matters progress, however, it becomes apparent that the teachers' preferences and judgments are prevailing. This can happen explicitly and overtly, but is more likely to be done insidiously. Indeed, there are some teachers (I have sat in their classes) who vigorously deny that any subtle manipulation of events is occurring, even as they express surprise that the "collaborative" curricula to be studied and the methods to be used coincidentally happen to match those that they prefer.

*Be Ready to Admit Your Errors.* Learners seem to warm to teachers who acknowledge that they don't have all the answers and that, like their students, they sometimes feel out of control. So be prepared to admit to being plagued by occasional feelings of anxiety and unease about the inadequacies you perceive in yourself. Such admissions will help reduce the tension students feel about their own need to be seen as perfect by their peers and teachers.

Remember, however, that your admissions of error only have some kind of releasing effect on students when they are made after you have already established a degree of credibility. The timing of such admissions of error is all important. If you walk into a classroom and begin immediately to assert your inadequacy without having previously established that you have something to offer students, you will probably be perceived as overwhelmingly weak or inept. In fact, the typical reaction from most students will be annoyance at having found themselves in a class where they obviously aren't going to learn anything.

So, whereas public declarations of fallibility from

teachers who have clearly earned credibility are prized by students, these same declarations from teachers who are unknown quantities may produce an effect exactly opposite to the one intended. Instead of releasing students from the self-imposed burden of needing to be exemplars at whatever activities they are exploring, it increases their burden of anxiety. In response to teachers' ill-timed avowals of inadequacy, students might quite legitimately ask, "Well, if you have so little to offer me, then why on earth am I here?"

*Reveal Aspects of Yourself Unrelated to Teaching.* Be ready to refer to enthusiasms, passions, and concerns outside your teaching role. When you reveal aspects of your personhood, it gives students a sense that they're dealing with a flesh-and-blood human being. Tarule (1988) calls this the autobiographical metaphor in teaching and points out how women, in particular, warm to teachers who are willing to bring evidence of their own extracurricular enthusiasms into the classroom.

For many years I steadfastly refused to refer to anything to do with my life outside the classroom. To me, personal disclosure smacked of amateur psychotherapy and indicated only that the teacher was using the learning group as a dumping ground for unresolved personal issues. There is no doubt that this can sometimes happen, but the authentic disclosure that students appreciate is very far from this. It is seen in teachers using incidents from their own daily lives to illustrate general principles, in their talking about the passions that led them to develop an interest in their fields, and in referring to the enthusiasms that currently sustain and renew these interests.

*Show That You Take Students Seriously.* Listen carefully for any concerns, anxieties, or problems voiced by students. If none are forthcoming, arrange opportunities and provide encouragement for students to speak out about what's on their minds. When concern is expressed on an issue—no matter how misplaced or trivial it seems to you—don't give a quick and polished response and then move on to something else. Give students plenty of time to express their thoughts. Don't finish their sentences for them. Don't rephrase what they've just told you as a way of benevolently interpreting their anxieties for them. You may feel that you're saving them some embarrassment by doing this, but in reality you're sending them the humiliating message that you don't think they are capable of speaking intelligently for themselves.

Be wary of your actions unwittingly reinforcing students' belief that they are incapable of contributing to discussion at any serious level. Even if you're confused about what someone is saying or impatient to ask a series of sharp, quick questions for clarification, resist these temptations. Hold yourself back, and the chances are that another class member will jump in and state the same concern in a way that is clearer to you. Here is Ira Shor's attempt to show students he takes them seriously:

> I modulate my voice to conversational rhythms rather than didactic, lecturing tones. I listen intently to every student utterance and ask other students to listen when one of their peers speaks. I don't begin my reply after the student ends his or her *first* sentence, but ask the student to say more about the question. If I'm asked what I think, I say I'd be glad to say what I think but why don't a few more people speak first to what the student just said, whether you agree or not. If I don't have a reply to what a student said, or don't understand a series of student comments, and can't invent on the spot questions to reveal the issue, I go home and think about it and start a next class from what a student said before, to keep signalling to students the importance of their statements [Shor and Freire, 1987, p. 117].

Be ready to explain, clearly and frequently, why you wish students to do the things you are asking. If students propose alternatives to your carefully thought-out plans, don't dismiss them out of hand. If you need time to think about a student's suggestion, then say this and promise to respond at the next class—and keep this promise. Be open to change. Show your readiness to negotiate and to adapt what you had planned to some other format. When students suggest themes, exercises, and issues they wish to explore, even if these are outside the scope of your original activities, consider very seriously how you can make some compromise to include some of these. If, in good faith, your own convictions or external constraints make these inclusions impossible, be prepared to explain and justify your decisions. Don't fall back on your presumption of authority as a way of winning the day, and don't imply that students lack the sophistication needed to understand your reasoning by refusing to discuss it with them.

*Don't Play Favorites.* In every class there are students whom you like more than others, people whose work you look forward to receiving, and people whom you would welcome as personal friends. Conversely, there are those whom you dislike personally, whom you think boorish and insensitive, and whom you believe are sliding through a course with a minimum of effort and a maximum of cynical contempt. You wouldn't be human if you didn't warm to some students as people and freeze in the presence of others. But if you are ever to be trusted by students, it is absolutely essential that you don't allow yourself the luxury of exercising these personal dislikes, that you avoid playing favorites.

Playing favorites—showing that you regard some people's work more favorably because of their appealing personalities and that you are prejudiced against others' efforts for their personal failings—destroys your credibility in students' eyes very quickly. So watch out that in discussions you don't slip into the habit of giving automatic preference to the contributions of those you like, while only acknowledging as a last resort the contributions of those you dislike. Try not to let your nonverbal gestures communicate how you feel about the personalities of contributors to discussions. Be alert to students' picking up your nonverbal messages about which students you like or dislike personally. When you see students making scapegoats of people whom you personally dislike, ask yourself how much your attitude is coming through to the group. When you see scapegoating happening, send a strong symbolic message by explicitly creating a space in the discussion where the person who was made the scapegoat has the chance to contribute—fully and freely—without intimidation. You are bound to have likes and dislikes regarding the different students in your classes. The important thing is to avoid letting these influence your public actions as a teacher.

***Realize the Power of Your Own Role Modeling.*** Teachers sometimes shy away from acknowledging the significance of their own actions to students. They believe that regarding their own actions as particularly significant within a learning group indicates an unpleasant egoism. They like to think that they are at one with students and that their own actions have no more significance than those of any other member of the learning group. This is patently not the case. As Jackson (1986) acknowledges, the role modeling undertaken by teachers is the most important element in transformative teaching. What we do as teachers is invested with enormous symbolic significance by students. So recognize the inevitable symbolic significance of your actions and make a virtue of necessity by ensuring as far as you can that these actions are perceived as authentic by students.

Let me give an example from my own practice of how seriously I take role modeling as a contributing component to trust building. My primary function as a teacher is to encourage critical thinking—something I suspect is an organizing principle for teachers across many academic disciplines and subject boundaries. More than any other factor, it is a teacher's willingness to display the habits of critical questioning towards his or her own ideas and actions that encourages these same habits in students.

From my own practice, I know that the position of

institutional authority I possess as a professor at Teachers College or as the "expert" consultant invited to give a keynote speech or conduct a workshop means that most people will be reluctant to criticize publicly any of my pronouncements. The risk of doing this is perceived as just too great. When they recall how such criticism has been received by leaders in the past, they may conclude that silence is the best policy or that, if they do speak, it should be to affirm the validity and accuracy of the leaders' insights.

Knowing this, I usually critically scrutinize my own ideas in front of my students or conference audiences. I will talk about mistakes I have made, about errors in my work, or about times when I wrote about something before fully understanding the phenomenon. I will discuss the areas of my work most in need of refinement. I will identify the issues I wish I had paid attention to or the most problematic areas for future inquiry. I talk about my confusions as much as my certainties. It is easier for me to do this without damaging my credibility than for someone just beginning in the field. Because of my writings and speeches and the credibility that accrues to published authors (regardless of whether what they published actually made any sense), I can move very quickly to this critical role modeling. Were I back in 1970 teaching my first classes, I would be much more cautious about this approach.

One thing I am very careful to do is to encourage the first hesitant critical comments of students, even if I think their criticisms are wholly misconceived. Despite my annoyance at being personally criticized, I try to make sure that the giver of this criticism is not silenced by other members of the group anxious to observe what they see as the pedagogical proprieties of the college classroom. A very powerful symbolic action for me is to distribute to students copies of reviews critical of my books and to point to the valid points in such reviews. This is a difficult thing for me since I react to such reviews personally and with a sense of injured martyrdom. But if it were easy for me to distribute critical reviews, then the symbolic power of doing this would be diminished. Because it's obvious that I'm hurt by these reviews, students are that much more convinced that I mean what I say about being open to criticism.

Shor describes, in similar terms, how he acts carefully to model the critical thinking he tries to encourage in students:

> What I try . . . is to demonstrate that there is no punishment for disagreeing with me, and also there is no reward for simply agreeing with me. I do this in several ways. In class, I react blankly to any student who mimics my ideas in his or her own voice. I do not model approval of mimicry. Then, I raise questions about my very own position, phrased by the student, to challenge their manipulation of me for a grade. If students write papers mimicking my ideas, I do the same thing, but in written response on their essays, asking leading questions about the ideology they "psyched out." I don't give automatic As to the mimic-papers and my written questions urge the student to reason out the issues in depth, next time. From the reverse point of view, if a student writes a paper or makes a statement antagonistic to my views, I don't pounce on him or her in a one-to-one debate. Instead, I reproduce the paper for class reading and discussion, or re-present the statement as a problem-theme for our inquiry [Shor and Freire, 1987, p. 184].

Teachers who declare that they are running critical or liberatory classrooms in which everything is open to critical scrutiny cannot expect students to breathe an immediate sigh of relief and release at inhaling this heady air' of intellectual freedom. The more likely reaction is for students to wonder exactly which particular game the teacher is playing and when his or her agenda will start to emerge. So if you're trying to encourage critical thinking, you must expect a period in which students will scrutinize very carefully to what degree your protestations are congruent with your actions.

## Balancing Credibility and Authenticity

Credibility and authenticity are elusive concepts, made the more so by the fact that they cannot be easily standardized. It is impossible to develop training packages to tell people how to be credible or authentic, since contextual features affect so strongly how students and teachers define credible and authentic behaviors. The most one can do is offer some of the general guidelines discussed in this chapter, give examples of how teachers in different settings try to build trust, and urge teachers to pay attention to the necessity for doing this. However, although these concepts evade precise definition, students sense when they are and are not present. In fact, it is usually much easier to say when these elements are absent, since students are mistrustful and uneasy, and their awareness of these feelings is sharp and disturbing. When students trust teachers, they cross new intellectual terrain with a tread that is firm and confident. When they mistrust teachers, each step is filled with trepidation and taken with the ever-present fear that it will be the one to send them sinking into quicksand or hurtling into a ravine.

The problem with pursuing authenticity and credibility (aside from the fact that neither of these concepts can be standardized in behavioral terms) is that the actions associated with these ideas often seem contradictory. In pursuing one you risk threatening the other. On the one hand, in striving to establish your credibility with students, you risk seeming to show off your knowledge and experience in a manner that appears authoritarian, arrogant, and inauthentic. On the other hand, however, in striving to be authentic, you risk weakening your credibility if you overdo your readiness to admit to error; students can be left with a perception that your most distinguishing characteristic is your ineptness. You also strain your credibility when you make students squirm in embarrassment because you are too personally revealing about your life outside the classroom. No student likes a teacher to use a class as a therapy group for the exorcising of his or her personal demons. So overemphasizing or mistiming can destroy the very trust you are working so hard to create.

This problem has no easy solutions, and most of the time you will probably feel you are erring too much on one side or the other. The only comfort I can give is this. If you don't make the effort to build credibility or act authentically, then you will do more harm than good. Better to try and achieve some sort of balance, knowing this will always remain elusive, than to neglect this trust building entirely. Teaching is never easy, and of all the complex balances we try to attain, being credible and authentic in the right proportions is one of the most difficult. But if you neglect entirely the need to build credibility in students' eyes, then they will have little confidence in the value of what you ask them to do. And if you behave inauthentically, they will regard your asking them to do it as a self-serving confidence trick.

# CHAPTER THIRTEEN

# Dealing with the Political Realities of Teaching

In the mind of the lay public, one of the images most frequently associated with college teaching is that of the ivory tower. The practice of education is often thought of as being cut off from the mainstream of society and pursued by high-minded ascetics ensconced in a tower of pure thought situated far above the grubby realities of daily life. Alternatively, colleges and universities are thought of as refuges for those crippled individuals too frail to participate in the maelstrom of normal existence. Teaching is often regarded by the business world as a shielded occupation suitable chiefly for those unable to survive the harsh necessities of commercial life. David Lodge's novel *Nice Work* (1989) captures very well this division between academic and business life.

A common apothegm about education, including teacher education, maintains that "those who can't do—teach, and those who can't teach—teach teachers." Shielded from the nastiness of life, teachers are often regarded by nonteachers as living above political pressures. Nothing could be further from the truth. Political processes, pressures, and constraints constantly make themselves felt, both inside and outside the classroom.

## The Political Dimensions of College Teaching

Teaching is infused with political significance. Despite the popularity of the ivory tower metaphor, college teachers do

177

not practice their craft in a cocoon insulated from political realities. Instead, they have to deal with a number of political factors that affect whether and how they teach. How one gets and keeps a job is partly a political matter. Those academics who have cultivated a network of influential contacts while still in graduate school and who have researched the culture of the field in which they seek employment are much more likely to know what they need to do and whom they need to contact to find work.

The politics of the college classroom and staff room, so graphically depicted in C. P. Snow's novel *The Masters* (1951), are ubiquitous. Few teachers can avoid at some time becoming embroiled in political battles that spring from, or are exacerbated by, personality conflicts. Getting tenure is as much a political as an academic process, involving teachers in researching the culture of their institutions. They must know which of the holy trinity of tenure criteria (scholarship, teaching, service) really matter. They have to find out which opinions are allowed to be voiced and which bring one's "soundness" into question. They need to discover which journals are the most highly regarded within the college so that they can target their work towards these. (Journals are like baseball cards—you can trade three articles in a less prestigious one for one article in a leader in the field.) They must know which figures in the institution have sufficient political clout (and have made few enough enemies) to be able to speak safely in support of their candidacy in tenure committees.

When a large grant is awarded by a foundation or corporation to a college or university, the scramble by departments and individuals to obtain pieces of this sometimes makes Machiavelli seem fainthearted and overly scrupulous. If more than one department or program is competing for a single new position that has just been approved, the lobbying and infighting that occurs in response is as vicious and frantic as any seen on Capitol Hill. When teachers face budget cuts and know that one department or program within the institution must be cut or removed entirely to save the rest, then things really start to heat up. In committees, issues one might believe would be debated purely on academic grounds—such as whether a new program should be approved, whether an assessment procedure should be changed, or whether a new teaching approach should be introduced—often become political conflicts fought against the backdrop of the participants' memories of past victories and defeats and of the hurts suffered during these.

In a broader context, political changes and processes all have their effects in the classroom. Changes in government or sudden shifts in national, regional, or local policy often mean that teachers lose or gain jobs and that public educational institutions stay open or close. The ascendancy to power of a new national political leader determined to make his or her political mark in the shortest possible time can have enormous effects inside the college classroom. In many presidential campaigns, college education is liable to be blamed for the country's economic decline or lauded as a national treasure. Battles over tenure, hiring, and firing are sometimes long and bloody, dividing not only faculty but also sections of the surrounding community.

Additionally, what one is allowed to teach and how one is allowed to teach it are matters over which college teachers are often the last to exert any control. If governments decide that some subjects are of greater importance to economic growth or ideological socialization than others, then these economically productive or ideologically sound subjects invariably receive preferential funding. What proportion of the curriculum should be taken up by different disciplines, what comprises a national or core curriculum, whether breadth or depth should be favored, how cultural literacy is defined, whether certain minorities are discriminated against or unfairly favored—all these issues are subject to guidelines and legislation developed by people who have never taught in a college classroom. So the microcosmic worlds of classrooms and staff rooms are hardly insulated from the political conflicts raging outside. As Shor (1986) shows, educational institutions are prime battlegrounds for the "culture wars" fought in the wider society.

## Strategies for Political Survival

Political survival involves the ability to negotiate and retain the physical resources, fiscal support, and institutional credibility necessary to work with students in a positive, affirming manner. The various insights and skills related to political survival as a college teacher are not codified as part of the accepted body of knowledge in teacher education. They are learned on the job. Many of these skills and insights are contextually specific, applying only to one specific college setting. However, some general advice applies across collegial contexts.

Most teachers work in colleges in which power plays and shifting organizational priorities affect how they practice their craft. New college teachers are often hired on temporary contracts with no guarantee of renewal. Junior instructors and untenured faculty exist in a limbo of professional uncertainty on the margins of their institutions. Existing on the margins of institutions can be exhilarating and creative in times of economic prosperity. In times of austerity, however, it can soon become debilitating and demoralizing. So a degree of tactical shrewdness and an appreciation of the need to pay attention to strategy are political necessities for college teachers.

*Talk to Your Colleagues.* It is vital to talk with your colleagues about the unofficial criteria governing reappointment, promotion, and tenure, as well as about the implications of the criteria contained within official policy statements. You need to find out, and to let others know, whose voices have credibility within the institution and who controls its vital functions. For example, making enemies of administrative and support staff early on can wreck the most brilliant pedagogic initiatives. If you turn up for class to find your room has been assigned to someone else, the video camera you booked has not arrived, and there is no heat, then the most detailed and sophisticated models of practice are rendered irrelevant.

You need to talk to colleagues who have been teaching for a while about the patterns of informal and formal communication within the organization. Those who have formal positions of organizational responsibility are not always those who possess the most influence. So share with your colleagues, and ask them to discuss with you, strategies for dealing with financial crises, with attacks by unsympathetic external groups, and with administrative attempts to render your educational efforts meaningless. By discussing these issues, you increase your chances of building a network of supportive contacts. It is not just students who need a sustaining community of peers to survive higher education. For many of the same reasons this is just as important for college teachers. As Freire declares, "Acting alone is the *best* way to commit suicide" (Shor and Freire, 1987, p. 61).

Since talking about the political culture of an institution does not always come easily to those working within it, you might want to try encouraging your colleagues to participate in some exercises designed deliberately to foster these conversations. The following small-group exercises might be useful to you as a way of starting the process of talking with colleagues about the political realities of college teaching. These exercises can also be used with groups of teachers from different institutions as a way of generating some broad rules of thumb for political survival.

### Critical Incident Exercise: Threat and Response

After forming into groups of four, think back to a time when you felt threatened by political developments within your institution. Briefly describe this episode, making sure to include information about the nature of the threat, where and when this was felt, who was involved in the episode as friends and enemies, how you responded to the threat (what worked for you and what backfired), and the consequences of this experience for your career as a teacher and your own emotional survival.

After recording these details individually, come together

to compare and collate your individual accounts. Try and identify similarities in the nature of the threats faced and the responses made. If some basic rules of thumb for political survival emerge, make sure you note these down. If common mistakes, miscalculations, and political errors are evident, note these down as well.

*Memorandum Exercise: Political Survival*

Imagine that this is your last day in the job you currently occupy. An acquaintance of yours, whom you wish well, is coming in from outside to take over your position. Unfortunately, you are unable to meet this person before he or she takes up your former duties.

Write a confidential memorandum to your successor titled "Rules of Political Survival." This memo should contain your advice and observations about basic rules of political survival within your organization that you have developed as a result of your experiences over the years. This advice might include (but is not restricted to) your judgments of political pitfalls to be avoided, the informal channels of communication or power structures that exist, the cultural taboos you've noticed, the symbolic terms, concepts, and ideas that are never challenged, and possible allies or enemies.

After you have written this memorandum in private, come together with three other people to exchange information and experiences. Read your memorandums to one another and compare and collate your accounts. Try to identify common rules for political survival as well as common pitfalls to be avoided.

***Know Your Enemy.*** College teachers often see themselves as change agents within hostile cultures. They are inspired with a reformist zeal and want to ensure that their college's treatment of students is characterized by compassion, equity, and justice. If this is your situation, it is important that you ensure that your efforts carry the lowest risk to yourself while producing the greatest effect for those you are trying to help.

A common tactical error teachers commit is that of destroying their credibility early on in their history at a college. For example, they will attend their first faculty meeting and denounce the administration for its shortsightedness, bureaucratic inflexibility, and implicit propagation of racist propaganda. The reactions to this outburst displayed by faculty with longer histories at the institution may vary from amusement to suspicion, weariness, or resentment. They may stereotype the reformist teacher as a knee-jerk radical who took too many drugs in the 1960s. Those in positions of power who are hostile to these criticisms will quietly make a mental note that in two year's time the teacher's contract will expire and that there is no legal requirement for its renewal.

A basic rule of survival as a change agent in hostile territory is to know your enemy. If, as a junior member of an organization, you wish to persuade those in power of the validity of ideas and proposals that are unfamiliar and threatening to them, you need to couch these in accessible terms. One way to do this is to learn the language, both explicit and symbolic, spoken by those in power. It is surprising how much you can accomplish with no one objecting or even noticing, if you describe your activities in language and symbolic terms that are familiar and approved.

So if you're a new teacher in an unfamiliar and perhaps hostile environment, I would advocate spending the first six months keeping your eyes and ears open and your mouth shut. Use this time to draw a political map of the institution, to chart the organizational power lines. Immerse yourself in the organizational culture and penetrate its symbolic system. This experience will be invaluable in helping you to choose the best time to take a stand on an issue you feel is important, but one you know will not be well received by those in power.

Not only will this period of immersion help you to choose the most opportune time to make a stand, it will also help you to frame your stance so that it has the greatest organizational effect and the least professional and personal cost to yourself. There are, of course, occasions when keeping your mouth shut is liable to do little other than to bolster the position of those hostile to your ideas. But there are many other times when watching and learning are the necessary precursors to acting. Shor describes his attitude to doing this as follows:

> Now, I see better the value of research and preparation, to make opposition count, and also as a way of reducing mistakes and unnecessary risks. If you do a careful institutional profile, a map of who is on what side politically, then you can find allies, scout your enemies in advance, get a feel for what terrain offers some political opening. This preparation not only reduces the chances of miscalculating the room for opposition, but it also starts knitting you into your location. I found that I had to learn what the history of politics had been in my college before I arrived there as a new professor. It's very easy to discredit yourself if you stand up naively and propose something that had been just fought over before you arrived [Shor and Freire, 1987, p. 66].

One very practical piece of additional advice given by Shor on this matter concerns the importance of teachers earning deviance credits. Shor describes this process as "taking on some of the harmless tasks of the institution so that you get recognized as a legitimate part of the scenery" (Shor and Freire, 1987, p. 66). Deviance credits are institutional kudos, brownie points earned by performing the approved tasks necessary to organizational functioning, such as serving on college alumni committees or helping to organize fund-raising events. Undertaking such tasks earns people credibility as organizational loyalists. Consequently, when it comes time for them to take an oppositional stance, they cannot be dismissed as troublemakers disloyal to the institution. Their voice carries with it the credibility accrued from their having performed organizationally approved tasks. Because their activities have earned them a reputation as organizational loyalists, attention is paid to their concerns. In effect, they cash in the deviance credits they have logged up over the preceding months.

*Build External Alliances.* In fighting organizational battles, it is easy to focus all your attention on internal foes and obstacles and forget the world outside. Yet one of the greatest assets teachers can bring to bear in support of their internal activities is that of external recognition. When an organization knows that a particular program is recognized and approved by institutions and individuals outside that organization, then teachers working within that program are less dispensable and their activities are viewed as more significant. It is obviously important to build alliances within the organization and to let those in power know of the successes and achievements of your program. But nothing disturbs administrators so much as knowing that if a program is cut or closed or if a teacher is sacked, there will be an outcry from institutions and individuals outside the organization.

My own career as an educational author stemmed from precisely this awareness of the importance of external recognition. At one institution, I faced great pressure to cut the educationally valuable but financially negligible community services I was overseeing. As a way of gaining external attention for these, I began to write articles for educational journals describing these community services. Since many of these activities focused on nontraditional forms of education, such as a free educational advisory service, a home study service, a learning to learn program, and an autonomous learning groups scheme (Brookfield, 1985b), editors seemed ready to feature articles documenting these initiatives within different American and British journals of educational practice.

I also made an effort to contact local and national educational journalists to let them know about the coverage these initiatives were receiving in journals in the United States and Britain. This resulted in features on and mentions of my work in local and national papers as well as a local radio interview. This may all sound somewhat self-aggrandizing and media savvy, but at the time it was a sheer survival necessity. It did not prevent the closure of my program and the college, but I believe it brought me a breathing space in which I could rethink my next move.

I am not suggesting that every college teacher become a cultivator of journalists and turn into a prolific author. The external alliances you choose to build and the strategies you employ in building them will depend on your particular context. But you do need to pay attention to this dimension of external support and to realize that your survival as a teacher may depend partly on who is prepared to support you from outside the institution when you are facing difficulties on the inside. In *The Corridors of Power* (1964) C. P. Snow declared that a nose for danger was the most useful attribute people needed to survive politically within organizations. For me, having a nose for danger has led me to formulate Brookfield's law of employment—every job you take you should expect, eventually, to be fired from, which means that from day one you should be building external alliances as protection against the day someone fires you.

*Choose Your Battles Carefully.* As teachers with limited resources and precarious positions, we need to choose our battles carefully. We need to know when to bend and when to stand firm. We need to realize that it is easier to get through an apparently impenetrable brick wall by finding the stones with the least mortar around them and chipping away at these weak areas rather than by trying to push the whole wall over. We need to recognize that it may sometimes be best to skirt round the wall rather than to try and force our way through. You only have so much energy. The energy expended in surviving and celebrating the inchoate diversity of classroom life is enormous and often leaves little over for fighting struggles outside. So the struggles you choose have to be significant and, if possible, to contain within them the prospects of success or at least of progress.

I believe there are times and situations in which it's best to say, "There is very little I can do about this right now, so I may as well recognize this fact and use my energies for something I *can* do something about." Or, to say, "These circumstances mean that I can either live with an unsatisfactory situation or get out of teaching. So I may as well live with these circumstances as best I can, doing what little I can to change them, but mostly conserving my energies for a later date when change will be possible." Such an accepting attitude is, admittedly, not always possible and may only be a comfortable rationalization for cowardice. Sometimes there are clear-cut situations where moral imperatives mean that you have to fight a battle even with little hope of success. But in many other situations, teachers fail to choose their battles wisely and thus waste their energies by individually battling immovable forces to achieve little other than a fruitless martyrdom noticed by no one but themselves.

## The Political Value of Teaching

The essence of teaching and learning is change, and change always has political dimensions. For teachers and students, nothing is exactly the same after an educational event as it was before. Making a dent in the world is the inevitable consequence of teaching. You cannot teach without in some way changing yourself, your students, and the world around you. Trying to avoid changing others while you teach is like trying to walk on a bright sunny day without casting a shadow. As a teacher, the question you must answer is not whether or not you cast shadows (for you cannot avoid doing this) but what form these shadows take and on whom they fall. Sometimes teachers seek to escape their shadows by espousing the aims of students' "growth" and "development" as if these were somehow neutral processes that did not need specifying in moral, social, or political terms. But growth and development must always be to some end. Growth cannot occur in a vacuum. Nothing develops in a directionless way.

Most teachers who subscribe to ideas of helping students grow and develop have strong implicit ideas of what growth and development should lead to and look like. For example, they would probably resist the idea that it is legitimate to help people grow into stronger bigots. Or, that people should be helped to develop their capacities for abuse and exploitation. They would regard activities that taught people to believe that they were innately superior to all other races, classes, and cultures as antithetical to the spirit of college education. So most college teachers would recognize that certain directions are inherently antieducational. In such a recognition lies the awareness that teaching is inevitably infused with moral, social, and political ideals (Tom, 1984).

All educational activities, whether we admit this or not, stem from our idea of what a properly educated person looks like. Having a prescriptive moral ideal—a vision of what comprises a "fulfilled," "mature," or "healthy" person—is normal (Goodlad, Soder, and Sirotnik, 1990). Although teachers may not often realize it, most of them believe in values such as fairness, equal opportunity for participation, honesty, freedom of expression, compassion, and respect. If you showed college teachers a classroom in which some students were consistently excluded from participation, publicly humiliated for their lack of progress, or punished for disagreeing with the received wisdom, these practices should generally be condemned.

Tell these same teachers, however, that their condemnation has a moral and political dimension to it, and they would probably deny this. Yet, fairness, equality, honesty, freedom, compassion, and respect for others are unmistakably moral and political values. They are central to the democratic tradition. Just as we would condemn a political process in which certain groups were excluded or humiliated, so we must condemn an educational process in which these things are happening. So, what we consider good teaching and who we regard as good teachers are judgments that rest, very frequently, on the application of democratic criteria. Whether we choose to recognize it or not, the values of college teaching are democratic political values.

## The Political Purposes of Teaching

College teaching is a political activity, in both the broad and the narrow sense of the word *political*. A political activity encourages people to ask awkward questions about why things are the way they are, whose interests these arrangements serve, and how things might be different. In a political activity, people challenge the accuracy and legitimacy of those issues and problems defined as important and sometimes substitute their own issues and problems. Any time teachers encourage students to think in different ways, to explore alternative interpretations of their experiences, or to challenge the accuracy and validity of society's "givens," then their teaching must, in this sense, be considered political.

Hence, the main political purpose of teaching is not to transmit a particular ideology; instead, it is to help students develop a critically alert cast of mind. Any class in which standardized syllabuses are abandoned because of their evident artificiality or in which officially prescribed criteria of excellence are discarded because they do not suit the context is a political class. Any teacher who encourages students to question the pronouncements of experts and to trust their own insights and judgments when their experience confirms these—even when they are contradicted by officially defined norms and standards—is a political teacher. Almost any subject can be taught politically if your teaching encourages students to question accepted criteria of performance and to identify the contextual origins of these criteria.

Another important reason for teaching is to help students develop a greater sense of agency in their lives. Having a sense of agency allows one to be a creator of events as much as a reactor to them. It enables one to construct one's own meanings and to live by these, rather than having them constructed by someone else. Creating these meanings occurs through the arduous process of testing our emerging insights and understandings against our experiences. Classrooms are one of the settings where people can do this without needing to fear where this process of meaning making may take them.

One of the most politically significant things that can happen in a college classroom is when students realize that various ideas, bodies of knowledge, and interpretive perspectives they had always regarded as forbidden territory are finally open to them. Many college students return to education in adult life with a history of school experiences in which their self-esteem was systematically and brutally assaulted. When these students find that their experiences are taken seriously, that their opinions are listened to and respected, and that their interpretations of the world are subjected to the same serious analysis as those of the teacher, enormous changes in self-concept can occur. When students sense that they matter in the classroom, they come to believe that their ideas and wishes should count in arenas of life other than academe. If people who have previously defined themselves as educational failures feel that they are valued and respected in college classrooms, then their enhanced feelings of self-worth can provide the affective underpinning of profound attempts to change aspects of their personal, occupational, and political lives.

Inevitably, the meanings students make and the consequences these have for their lives sometimes diverge from mainstream, traditional values. Teachers who encourage in students the process by which such divergent meanings are developed are themselves likely to incur the wrath of those guarding dominant cultural values. Because students who acquire a critically alert cast of mind are likely to ask awkward questions of people in positions of power and because such students will mistrust simplistic solutions, political slogans, and blatant propaganda, their activities have consequences for their teachers. Teachers who encourage students to create their own meanings rather than accepting those that are culturally or politically prescribed run the risk of receiving public criticism (and in some societies much worse) from the politically powerful.

The political nature of teaching is perhaps most dramatically illustrated by the numbers of teachers and scholars who are routinely tortured and murdered because they foster critical questioning. In some societies the worst that can happen to teachers who encourage students to question official definitions of issues and problems and to ask whose interests curricula serve is that they are publicly criticized or that they get fired. In other societies, teaching that is divergent or critical of prevailing assumptions will result in imprisonment, exile, torture, or even death.

As I write these words, safe in my apartment eyrie overlooking Harlem, I know that across the world in regimes of the right and left teachers who challenge prevailing ways of thinking and acting are being tortured and murdered by police forces, the military, death squads, and vigilantes. Some educational institutions in less extreme societies also impose their own constraints on critical questioning, such as denial of promotion and tenure, inability to get one's work published, progressive isolation within one's institution, or ridicule for one's supposed eccentricities. So, rather than teaching being the last refuge of the naive or politically disinterested, it is actually one of the most intensely politicized occupations one can choose.

# CHAPTER FOURTEEN

# Some Truths About
# Skillful Teaching

Effectiveness as a concept has enormous appeal (Beidler, 1986; Brown and Atkins, 1987; Hoadley and Vik, 1989). It suggests that there are standardized practices that apply with equal relevance to every context within which teaching occurs. Were this true, then the world of college teaching would be much cleaner and simpler than it is in reality. All that new teachers would need to do would be to learn the simple rules of effective practice, acquire the necessary techniques, and go out into college classrooms and practice these. This would produce a cadre of practitioners, all doing the same things in the same way, and all of whom could be regarded as exemplars of effectiveness. The clarity, simplicity, and order of such a world is what many administrators and teachers yearn for, and were it to exist in reality, it would mirror perfectly the assumptions under which many colleges function.

Seeing effectiveness in this way, however, ignores the inchoate messiness of college teaching. The concept is decontextualized, thereby rendering it remote and irrelevant to teachers who are grappling with the dilemmas, distortions, and ambiguities of practice. Effectiveness is irrevocably contextual (Pratt, 1988b). What is effective in one context, with one student or group of students, or for one purpose may be severely disfunctional in another context, with different people, or for another purpose (Cervero, 1989).

192

Effectiveness is also irredeemably value-laden. The decision concerning what constitutes effectiveness rests on certain judgments and interpretations. Whenever one concept of effectiveness gains ascendancy over others, the power struggles between groups that are seeking to define this concept in their own ways are clearly evident. What are effective behaviors for one group of teachers may be examples of psychological bludgeoning for another. What one teacher may consider an effective teaching effort a student may see as a demeaning experience. So talking about effectiveness as if it were an objective concept whose features can be easily agreed on by all reasonable people is mistaken. We always have to ask, Effective for what? and Effective for whom?

In a sense, effectiveness is also a phenomenologically derived concept, one grounded in students' perceptions of what is happening to them and in the meanings they attach to these experiences. Equating effective teaching with how well teachers perform a previously defined set of behaviors risks neglecting entirely the effect these behaviors have on students, thus rendering the student's experience irrelevant.

To determine whether teaching is effective, we must, ultimately, see whether students are learning. Anything that helps students learn is good, effective teaching (Ericksen, 1984; Hayes, 1989). Anything that hinders their learning is ineffective teaching. Sometimes what most hinders students' learning is a teacher's determination to behave according to some well-defined notion of effectiveness. One example of how an uncritical, decontextualized application of a supposedly effective teaching behavior actually hinders learning can be taken from my own practice as a workshop leader.

As a workshop leader, I have used small-group methods for many years. Until a few years ago, I would typically announce a small-group task, set the groups to work, and then visit them in turn to see how they were doing. This continuous monitoring of small groups' progress was, so I was taught, an educationally effective way for a workshop leader to behave. Yet, as a learner, I was always irritated when a workshop leader would visit small groups as a supposedly objective, nonparticipating observer. Because we, as students, knew that the leader would eventually visit us to check on our progress, we would spend a lot of time surreptitiously watching him or her circling the room, anxiously waiting for our turn to perform. When the leader actually arrived at our group, we would change our behavior and play at being "good" students.

Essentially, we did our best to conform to what we thought the leader wished to see and to what would bring us his or her praise. We became obsessed with performing according to stereotyped ideas of good group participation, usually by raising the formality and frequency of our contributions the nearer the leader came to our group. Because we were concerned to show the leader how focused and task-oriented we were, any doubts we might have had about whether the problem addressed in the exercise was the real problem at hand were forgotten. Because raising questions about the validity of the task at hand was not what we were supposed to be doing, we would refrain from making our misgivings explicit for fear of being thought of as time-wasting dilettantes, unable to get down to the task at hand. After the leader had moved on to the next group, however, we would return to a more natural style of interaction, with as many pauses as contributions, and the critical questions we had been raising earlier would return to the fore.

This pattern of group behavior repeated itself in small-group exercises across contexts and disciplines. Gradually it began to occur to me that, far from focusing my attention in a fruitful way, the leader's visits were actually interfering with some significant learning. Under the pressure of needing to perform for the visiting leader, we were setting aside some important critical analysis. Instead of considering at length in whose interests it was that this particular problem be solved and what the definition of the problem said about the definer's values, we were anxiously waiting for our chance to show how animated, involved, and purposeful we were.

For this reason I have come to believe that after setting a small-group exercise the best thing I can do is to leave the groups alone. This shows them that I trust them enough to get on with what I'm asking, and it relieves them of the pressure of needing to prepare for my visit and then of performing for me. So, after announcing that I'm available to assist any group at any point in their deliberations, I take myself off to a corner of the room. Even though I have removed myself from direct involvement in the small groups' interactions, I am teaching effectively. I am making a contextual judgment about what helps people learn. Teachers have a curious mix of arrogance and well-meaning concern that often makes it difficult for them to conceive of how their absence can sometimes be an enhancement to learning. Yet, though this might seem bizarre or irresponsible, leaving students alone to get on with what you've asked them to do is often a very effective teaching action.

This chapter summarizes the chief themes of this book and offers specific advice on skillful teaching. The truths I present are applicable to the varied contexts in which college teachers teach and college students learn. All of them have been proposed, some more explicitly than others, in the foregoing chapters.

### Be Clear About the Purpose of Your Teaching

Develop a philosophy of practice, a critical rationale for why you're doing what you're doing. Possessing such an organizing vision will help you withstand those inevitable episodes when the puzzlement or opposition expressed at your efforts by students, colleagues, and administrators cause you to wonder whether you should continue teaching. Your vision will also help your students feel that they are under the influence of someone who is moved by well-thought-out convictions and commitments. Without a personal organizing vision we are rudderless vessels tossed around on the waves and currents of whatever political whims and fashions are prevalent at the time. Our practice may win us career advancement, but it will be lacking in the innate meaning that transforms teaching from a function into a passion.

Skillful teachers are critically responsive teachers. Although they are sensitive to contextual factors such as organizational necessities, students' experiences, and political climates, they have a clear rationale for their practice. The organizing vision for college teaching proposed in this book is the fostering of the critical thinking necessary for students to be able to reflect on the habitual assumptions underlying their actions and ideas. Such critical thinking is also central to building a democratic society with a political culture that is informed by values of freedom, fairness, justice, and compassion.

### Reflect on Your Own Learning

One of the best ways to improve your teaching is to experience, and to remember, what it feels like to learn something, especially something new and difficult. Reflecting on the experience of learning has some very powerful implications for your teaching. It will make you aware of the behaviors that affirm and encourage students and those that intimidate and hinder them. It will help you temper your criticism so that it is not interpreted as a personal assault on students. It will sensitize you to some of the typical rhythms of learning— such as incremental fluctuations and the attainment of learning plateaus—which will, in turn, prevent you from making needless and possibly harmful interventions. It will give you new insight into why and how people resist learning and what some useful responses to this resistance might be.

So, if you can, resolve to spend some time each semester, or even annually, in the role of a learner. Keep a learning journal of the highs and lows you experienced and what you think occasioned these. Then reflect on what these experiences mean for your own teaching.

Many of your intuitively developed ideas about teaching will probably be confirmed by this experience, but you may also be made aware of the unfortunate effects some of your habitual behaviors have on students. If you can, try to encourage the institution in which you work to mount a staff development effort in which teachers experience learning individually and then come together in reflective groups to consider the implications of these experiences for their own teaching.

## Be Wary of Standardized Models and Approaches

Teaching and learning are such complex processes, and teachers and learners are such complex beings, that no model of practice or pedagogical approach will apply in all settings. A lot of fruitless time and energy can be spent trying to find the holy grail of pedagogy, the one way to instructional enlightenment. No philosophy, theory, or theorist can possibly capture the idiosyncratic reality of your own experience as a teacher. Don't think that Freire, Dewey, Tyler, Rogers, or anyone else possesses the truth that fits your situation exactly.

You can draw much that is useful from the different models of practice that are available. But you should feel no compunction about rejecting elements of these, changing other parts of them before applying them in your practice, or abandoning them entirely when they don't fit. These models can be useful starting points, particularly when you're working in an unfamiliar context. But don't expect them to relieve you of the necessity to make endless judgments and choices about what works best and why. Making these judgments— sometimes rightly, sometimes wrongly—is the essence of teaching, and no generic model of practice will allow you to abdicate this responsibility.

## Expect Ambiguity

Participating in some teacher-training programs or reading some textbooks of practice can give you the idea that teaching is a rational, ordered process in which previously designed methods and curricula are put into practice to achieve expected outcomes. Organizations and licensing bodies need to operate on this assumption, or their whole raison d'être is called into question. But teachers quickly realize that teaching is often a journey into uncertainty in which they unlearn their reliance on standardized models and curricula.

As teachers we cross the borders of chaos to inhabit zones of ambiguity. For every event in which we feel things are working out as we anticipated they would, there is an event that totally confounds our expectations. It is difficult enough to predict what one person's response to a particular event will be, let alone to predict the responses of a group of students to the series of events we have planned in just one lesson unit. Contextual factors will distort the most perfectly planned curriculum or classroom project.

The one thing we can rely on with some certainty is that events will alter our neatly conceived plans. These events will sometimes be serendipitous, sometimes disastrous. But inevitably they will occur, so we need to learn to not be thrown by them. Remember that ambiguity is a given of college teaching, and that those who make this practice seem to be a flawless, seamless flow, are usually masters of pretense.

## Remember That Perfection Is Impossible

Expecting perfection in one's performance as a teacher will have one of three consequences: you will develop an ulcer in short order; you will become so demoralized at your inability to achieve perfection that you will leave teaching entirely; or you'll develop a cynical belief that your actions don't matter because nothing works anyway. Perfection in terms of one's personal performance is a chimera. You will never achieve it, and in pursuing it too unrealistically you will become so obsessed with your own actions that you'll forget the real reason for teaching—to help students learn.

Seeking perfection in pedagogic performance is as dangerously narcissistic as seeking perfection in sexual performance. In both situations, what is really important (what is happening to the other person) is forgotten as one becomes fixated on an idealized version of one's own perfection. So, while trying to be as responsive to students and as authentic in your actions as possible, you should never conclude that just because you fall short of your imagined ideal that what you are doing is worthless.

In terms of students' reactions to your efforts, you will rarely find that everyone with whom you are dealing thinks that what has transpired is somehow inspirationally transformative. Indeed, for every student who embraces change there will be one, or maybe more than one, whose energies will be wholly devoted to resistance. It is easy to become obsessed with these students who seem, stubbornly, to "refuse to grow" (Daloz, 1988) despite all your best efforts. But be wary of becoming obsessed with proving to yourself that you can be the perfect teacher by making even the most recalcitrant students become passionate advocates for your subject. Remember that no action you take will produce universally felicitous consequences. Every teaching choice is essentially a trade-off, entailing advantages and disadvantages. Try to learn to accept that if the overall advantages of one course of action outweigh its disadvantages, it is worth pursuing.

### Research Your Students' Backgrounds

Before beginning any educational effort, try and do as much research as you can on your students' backgrounds—their cultural values and allegiances; their experiences; their expectations; their language; and their most pressing concerns, problems, and dilemmas. If you can't do this before the educational activity begins, try your best to carve out some time in the first one or two sessions to explore these characteristics. You might want to think about using a variant on the critical incident technique along the lines that I've suggested at earlier points in the book.

To teachers impatient to get cracking on the important work of teaching, this research effort can seem like an indulgent waste of time. But if you are impatient about starting teaching, the chances are that this impatience grows out of a conviction that what you're teaching is important for students to know. And if you believe that something is important for students to know, then you're going to want them to take as much notice of it as possible and to see their learning as relevant and connected to their lives. If you neglect researching your students' backgrounds and cultures, however, you run several major risks. You risk turning them off you and your subject if you make a needlessly offensive remark or crack a hurtful joke without your realizing that you're doing this. You risk spending a lot of time preparing lectures that are delivered at a wholly inappropriate level or which fail to show any connections between your subject and your students' concerns. You risk producing materials and exercises that neither excite nor illuminate. You also risk creating at the outset a level of learner resentment and resistance that will take a long time to dismantle.

### Attend to How Students Experience Learning

A constant feature of your teaching should be a concerted effort to understand how students are experiencing learning. You can watch for nonverbal reactions, but these can be misinterpreted and there is a limit to how much they can convey. So take the time to include regular formative evaluation sessions in your classes, in which you ask for opinions on how things have seemed so far, what might be changed, what has failed to work, and so on. Try to get students to document their perceptions of learning in journals or through critical incident exercises. Encourage them to talk about their highs and lows and about the insights they are gaining into some of their rhythms of learning.

When you have some understanding of the most typical rhythms of learning and of how your actions are being perceived, try and think how you might make your practice more responsive to these features. It won't always be possible, or desirable, to make major adjustments. Not only will contextual constraints prevent this, but there will also be times when you have to make the judgment that while something appears problematic or puzzling to students as it is being experienced, it's your belief that its relevance will eventually become clear. But there will be other times when it is quite right to adjust what you're doing or to abandon it entirely in favor of something that connects more directly to students' experiences.

## Talk to Your Colleagues

Because college teachers spend so much of their time behind the closed doors of their classrooms, they can easily develop a sense of isolation and a distorted perception of their own dilemmas, problems, and failings. When teachers do talk to each other, their conversations often concern administrative necessities and procedures. Yet private and informal talks about varying responses they generate to crises and dilemmas can be enormously helpful.

The revelation that you are not the only person who sometimes feels that things are moving beyond your control can be enormously reassuring. It can help you avoid the emotional self-flagellation characteristic of those who engage in the quest for perfectability discussed earlier. The realization that your perceptions of your ineptitude and inadequacy are felt by other teachers about themselves generates an enormous sense of relief.

On a specific level, you can learn a great deal from listening to descriptions of how other teachers working in contexts similar to yours deal with the dilemmas, crises, and problems you yourself are facing. You can probably adapt some of their responses directly to your situation, as well as experimenting with variants on their strategies and tactics. One of the most effective staff development initiatives anyone in charge of faculty development can take is to release teachers from their normal duties and encourage them to talk to each other about their most pressing problems and dilemmas.

## Trust Your Instincts

Many teachers are socialized into believing that the knowledge and insights contained within textbooks and teacher-training programs have a greater legitimacy than the knowledge and insights they themselves generate in response to the particular crises and dilemmas of their own situations. Although textbooks and teacher education programs contain much that it useful (I write textbooks and teach in such a program so I have to believe this!), it is also true that teachers are the greatest experts in their own situations. No one is inside a crisis in exactly the way you are.

Very often teachers feel instinctively that a particular action is called for in a particular situation, but they refrain from following this instinct because it contradicts the theory espoused in teacher education programs. Textbooks can be right when teachers' instincts are wrong, but we should not always immediately assume that this is the case. If you feel strongly that something is right, even though it goes against conventional wisdom, be ready to acknowledge your instincts and act upon them.

Sometimes you will find that your instincts are completely wrong and that you have seriously miscalculated the consequences of following them. If this happens, then you will probably have learned how to recognize when your instincts are well grounded in reality. But don't automatically shut them off the first time they make themselves felt in the belief that if they don't match the theories espoused in teacher education then they must, by definition, be wrong.

## Create Diversity

Given the bewildering complexity of teaching and learning, a good rule of thumb is to use a diversity of materials and methods in your practice. This is important for two reasons. First, if you try out a range of materials and methods, there is a good chance that at some point in the activity the majority of students will find that their preferred learning style is being addressed. They will experience this as reassuring and affirming. Second, by introducing students to styles with which they are unfamiliar, you will be broadening their repertoires and helping them to flourish in a greater range of situations than would otherwise have been the case.

So, as you create diversity, try and mix visual with oral modes. Alternate small-group exercises with large-group plenaries. Blend active discussion and debate with opportunities for silent reflective analysis. Provide options within assignments for independent study and for group projects. Try out experiential learning techniques such as role play and simulation. Show films and make films.

Be particularly careful not to fall into habitual teaching patterns that grow out of your preferred learning style. For example, my own instinctive text dependence as a learner means that as a teacher I tend to underemphasize the use of visual aids and to forget the importance of depicting ideas graphically for students. By neglecting to do this I am severely hampering the learning of students who are visually attuned. Again, because I have a tendency to work independently on projects (I have never coauthored any of my published writings), I forget that many people much prefer working in teams and actually enjoy the interchange that sometimes seems an irritating waste of time to me. So I have to make a conscious effort to remind myself to curb my own tendency to hasten group processes that are inevitably time-consuming.

Of course, the diversity you employ as a teacher will be constrained by organizational variables, by students' levels of learning readiness, and by your own familiarity with the methods and materials involved. You can't be expected to change your style at the drop of a hat, particularly if it involves doing things with which you have no experience or training or which contradict fundamental aspects of your personality. For example, my own self-consciousness at not making an idiot of myself in front of people means that I have always found it difficult to participate in role plays. But most of us could probably inject a much greater degree of diversity into our teaching than is currently the case.

### Take Risks

Good teachers take risks in the full knowledge that these will not always work. They are ready to depart from planned curricula and methods if the moment seems to dictate this. The more you take risks, the more adept you become at recognizing when they are justified and likely to pay off. In particular, the better you become at responding to true teachable moments—those times when an unexpected event excites the interest and energy of a group in a way that had not been planned.

When these moments occur, it is important to build on them and use them to greatest effect. Often what you thought would be supremely exciting activities will draw responses of studied indifference from students, so you cannot afford to let the drama and theater of a true teachable moment slip away. Our teacher-training programs may have socialized us into avoiding departures from our syllabuses or lesson plans, and our organization may exhibit structural features that further inhibit this. But risking the exploration of unplanned and uncharted intellectual waters is often remembered by teachers and students as significant and exciting.

In this regard it is helpful to think of a good educational experience as being like a good conversation. Good conversations, by definition, cannot be predicted in advance. They are characterized by risk and spontaneity. If I knew what you were going to say before you said it, and if I could predict beforehand the turns my conversation with you would take, there would be no point in talking. Conversations characterized by this degree of predictability are experienced as forced and boring, and so is education. In contrast to some curriculum planners' beliefs that students must know in exact detail what is going to happen to them at each stage of the educational process, I advocate retaining some element of risk, surprise, and spontaneity.

### Recognize the Emotionality of Learning

Many educational textbooks and research reports use language and terminology that depict learning as an ascetic activity distinguished by rational inquiry. There are few recognizable flesh-and-blood human beings and little indication of the visceral ebbs and flows that accompany, and are intermingled with, the activity of learning. Yet, as students themselves report, learning is highly emotional. It involves great threats to students' self-esteem, especially when they are exploring new and difficult knowledge and skill domains. Even when they experience forward movement, there is likely to be a grieving for old ways of being and for lost assumptions. The emotional sustenance students receive from a supportive learning community is reported as crucial to their survival.

Being aware of the emotionality of learning is important for your practice. This awareness will help prepare you for the inevitable outpouring of anger and resentment that for some students accompanies the exploration of new intellectual areas. You will also be less likely to experience an angst-ridden scrutiny of your own apparent shortcomings, just because a student greets your activities with hostility rather than love. You will not rush to stem the process of grieving for old assumptions and identities but will see this as a natural accompaniment to change. You will also allow time for the expression of emotions that, if repressed, would fester until they represented a much larger block to learning than need be the case.

## Acknowledge Your Personality

One of the characteristics students value the most in their teachers is authenticity. If you teach in a way that belies fundamental aspects of your personality, you will come across as stilted and inauthentic. In particular, if you are introverted, quiet, and reflective, you should not try to pass yourself off as the pedagogic equivalent of Groucho Marx. Remember that many students will feel much more comfortable with you than with an outgoing, broadly gesturing extrovert. Remember also that the most charismatic of teachers can sometimes inhibit students as well as inspire them.

If you feel uncomfortable about behaving in a certain way, you should probably acknowledge to students and colleagues that this is the case. Be wary of becoming obsessed with exemplifying idealized behaviors that don't come naturally. For example, I find listening to students' questions and responding fully to these to be very hard work requiring great

concentration. To answer a complex question clearly, I need
to focus on my internal mental processes, almost to the exclusion of everything else. This means that I have no energy or
inclination left to spend on making eye contact with people
around the room. So when I'm listening to a question, I tend
to look only at the questioner. When I answer a question, I
will stare at the floor, focus on a spot in the middle distance,
or even close my eyes.

Now I know that in terms of "proper" classroom communication this is a terrible thing to do. But I also know that
if I'm to give a clear, articulate response to a question, it is
crucial for me to stop worrying about making eye contact
throughout the room. Were I to become obsessed with constantly rotating my head 180 degrees from left to right, right
to left, around the room, I would give a much more confused
response. So I will begin sessions with new groups by saying
that I find it difficult to think and look at the same time, so
they should not interpret my staring into space as implying
ignorance of their existence. In fact, it implies serious recognition of their existence, since it means I am struggling to
understand their questions as fully as possible and to give the
clearest answers I can.

### Don't Evaluate Only by Students' Satisfaction

Most of us go into teaching inspired by a desire to help others. And we often expect to be loved by our students for our
altruism. We may not always be aware of this expectation,
but for many people it constitutes a powerful assumption
that is implicit in much of their practice. One consequence
of this assumption is that when students greet our efforts
with anger and resentment, we immediately conclude that we
have somehow failed.

Hostile student evaluations of our practice are often
granted a credibility far greater than is actually merited. As a
teacher you need to remember that as students themselves
report, many of the significant learning episodes in their lives
are ones involving pain, anxiety, and challenge. While these

episodes are being experienced they may inspire resentment in students against the apparent cause of these emotions, that is, against you, the teacher. Knowing that the expression of such hostility might be interpreted as a sign of your pedagogic competence as much as a sign of your inadequacy is an important defense against the debilitating depression that often accompanies receiving a poor evaluation.

Additionally, you need to remember that much of the relevance of classroom activities is not appreciated by students until much later when they find themselves in contexts where what happened in the classroom suddenly fits the new situation. The fact that in the immediate aftermath of an activity students view their participation as irrelevant does not mean that you've wasted your time.

### Balance Support and Challenge

Of all the intractable dilemmas college teachers face in their practice, balancing support and challenge is one of the most problematic. Striving to achieve an equilibrium (ever-changing though this may be) between these two forces is crucial. The fundamental underpinning of all your actions as a teacher should be a respect for and affirmation of your students. If students feel they are in a hostile or indifferent environment, their commitment to learning will be seriously weakened. They may be physically present, but they will be mentally absent. Also, receiving criticism from teachers is experienced as psychologically devastating.

So keep in mind the fragile egos of your students and acknowledge the effort they have made, even if this effort has not produced the quality of work you would hope for. Remember that in their eyes your pronouncements carry enormous weight, and that a critical aside from you may be recalled for months, even years, as a deeply wounding experience. Leaven every oral and written criticism with praise, if at all possible.

But if students experience only affirmation and never challenge, then their encounter with you is not truly educational. Affirmation may be an important precondition of challenge, but it can never be considered the sum total of teaching. Without challenge, some students will never explore alternative perspectives, venture into new skill areas, or appraise critically the accuracy and validity of the habitual assumptions underlying their reasoning. Yet all these activities are central to developing the critical thinking that I believe is the fundamental purpose of college teaching across disciplines and contexts.

Achieving the right balance between challenge and support is difficult enough with one person in one task, let alone with a group of students pursuing multifarious activities. If you have to err on one side of the support-challenge equilibrium, I would advocate erring on the supportive side. When students receive affirmation from teachers whom they perceive as authority figures, the effect is astonishing. It is unfortunate, but true, that many students will only take their own ideas seriously after a teacher has validated them. By listening to and acknowledging students' voices, teachers can strengthen the shaky self-confidence of diffident learners and help them develop a sense of agency whether or not critical thinking occurs.

As Daloz (1988) remarks, to encourage learning means, literally, to encourage, to nurture in learners the strength and fortitude to confront what, to many, is a perilous and threatening journey. Since critical thinking represents such a journey for many students, they need to muster beforehand a formidable degree of courage, conviction, and strength. A period of support often provides the confidence that allows students to embark on this journey. Challenging conventional wisdoms and questioning previously accepted givens are intimidating prospects to students who have internalized the belief that their insights, skills, and experiences are not as valuable as the "official," "proper" knowledge contained in books and teachers' heads. So your affirmation of students can lay the psychological groundwork for subsequent critical thinking episodes.

## Recognize the Significance of Your Actions

You must always remember that your actions will be imbued with enormous symbolic significance by students. When it comes to the most crucial emotional interaction of all between teachers and students—that of building trust—teachers' actions count more than anything else. If your words and actions are seriously discrepant, then an air of artificiality will permeate the encounter.

Don't fool yourself into believing that merely by saying to students that you are all equal will make them view you as one of them. You can never escape the fact that your actions will be closely scrutinized for the messages students think they contain. Initiating a discussion and then staying silent, for example, will be perceived as a very significant action by students. They will ascribe all kinds of purposes to your silence and worry about the critical judgments that inform it. As Freire says "education is above all the giving of examples through actions" (Shor and Freire, 1987, p. 160). Knowing this, you can make a virtue of necessity and ensure that your actions model the kinds of intellectually demanding yet respectful behaviors you are seeking to encourage in students.

## View Yourself as a Helper of Learning

This is perhaps the simplest, yet the most profound, truth of all. The fundamental reason for teaching is to help someone learn something. Anything you do that contributes to this purpose is skillful teaching, no matter how much it may depart from your traditional expectations about how teachers are supposed to behave. Anything you do that inhibits learning, no matter how much it exemplifies traditional expectations, should be diminished or stopped. You have to make a judgment concerning what is realistic in this regard. For example, even if you feel that examinations inhibit rather than enhance learning, you generally can't avoid giving them. But when you reflect on your skill as a teacher, there is only one fundamental question you need to ask: Are my actions helping students learn?

Knowing that this is the fundamental criterion by which your efforts should be judged means that you can regard as skillful teaching many activities that fall well outside the traditional model of the teacher as charismatic performer. You can be a highly skillful teacher as a designer of well-conceived and provocatively experienced classroom exercises such as role plays and simulations. Being able to help students diagnose their difficulties within an area of study can be a very skillful teaching act, since understanding accurately the nature of these difficulties is crucial to addressing them. A teacher who arranges individual counseling with students to enhance their self-esteem or one who puts students in touch with others who have similar enthusiasms is also teaching effectively.

## A Final Note

Don't trust what you've just read. What for me are truths of skillful teaching may, for you, be partially or entirely inappropriate. Keep in mind that in the time between writing this manuscript and its publication I may have amended some of these truths, deleted others, and added still more. My continuing journey as a teacher through diverse contexts and dilemmas is bound to generate new insights. The one thing I can expect with certainty is surprise. So don't treat these insights as the final word on the quintessential truth about college teaching. For me to end this book claiming to offer a decontextualized, standardized package of teaching truths would be to contradict the critically reflective skepticism about such injunctions that I have been urging throughout the book.

Certainly I feel that these insights have some grounding in reality, or I would not have allowed them to be published with my name attached. I suspect that many readers will recognize parts of themselves and aspects of their own practice as they read this chapter. But don't think that if some element of your practice contradicts mine, yours must therefore be wrong. Listen to your nagging, inner voice. Be prepared to admit the possibility that your inner voice is right, even when all professional wisdom is to the contrary. Be ready to act on what your inner voice tells you, all the time knowing that periodically making mistakes is endemic to good teaching.

# References

Apple, M. W. *Education and Power.* New York: Routledge, Chapman & Hall, 1982.

Barer-Stein, H. M. "A Phenomenological Study of Adult Learners: Participants' Experiences of a Learner-Centered Approach." Unpublished doctoral dissertation, Department of Adult Education, Ontario Institute for Studies in Education, 1979.

Bates, H. M. "A Phenomenological Study of Adult Learners: Participants' Experiences of a Learner-Centered Approach." Unpublished doctoral dissertation, Department of Adult Education, Ontario Institute for Studies in Education, 1979.

Beidler, P. G. (ed.). *Distinguished Teachers on Effective Teaching.* New Directions for Teaching and Learning, no. 28. San Francisco: Jossey-Bass, 1986.

Belenky, M. F., Clinchy, B. M., Goldberger, N. R., and Tarule, J. M. *Women's Ways of Knowing: The Development of Self, Voice, and Mind.* New York: Basic Books, 1986.

Bligh, D. A. *What's the Use of Lectures?* Harmondsworth, England: Penguin, 1972.

Bligh, D. A. (ed.). *Teach Thinking by Discussion.* Philadelphia: Taylor & Francis, 1986.

Bloom, A. *The Closing of the American Mind: How Higher Education Has Failed Democracy and Impoverished the Souls of Today's Students.* New York: Simon & Schuster, 1987.

Boud, D. (ed.). *Developing Student Autonomy in Learning.* (2nd ed.) New York: Nichols, 1988.

Boud, D., and Griffin, V. (eds.). *Appreciating Adults Learning: From the Learner's Perspective.* London: Kogan Page, 1987.

Boud, D., Keogh, R., and Walker, D. (eds.). *Reflection: Turning Experience into Learning.* New York: Nichols, 1985.

Bourdieu, P., and Passerson, J. *Reproduction in Education, Society, and Culture.* Newbury Park, Calif.: Sage, 1977.

Bowles, S. B., and Gintis, H. *Schooling in Capitalist Society: Educational Reforms and the Contradictions of Economic Lifts.* New York: Basic Books, 1976.

Boyd, E. M. "Reflection in Experiential Learning: Case Studies of Counsellors." Unpublished doctoral dissertation, Department of Adult Education, Ontario Institute for Studies in Education, 1981.

Bridges, D. *Education, Democracy and Discussion.* Lanham, Md.: University Press of America, 1989.

Brookfield, S. D. "Independent Adult Learning." *Studies in Adult Education,* 1981, *13* (1), 15–27.

Brookfield, S. D. "Discussion as an Effective Educational Method." In S. H. Rosenblum (ed.), *Involving Adults in the Educational Process.* New Directions for Continuing Education, no. 26. San Francisco: Jossey-Bass, 1985a.

Brookfield, S. D. "Supporting Autonomous Adult Learning Groups." In S. D. Brookfield (ed.), *Self-Directed Learning: From Theory to Practice.* New Directions For Continuing Education, no. 25. San Francisco: Jossey-Bass, 1985b.

Brookfield, S. D. *Understanding and Facilitating Adult Learning: A Comprehensive Analysis of Principles and Effective Practices.* San Francisco: Jossey-Bass, 1986.

Brookfield, S. D. *Developing Critical Thinkers: Challenging Adults to Explore Alternative Ways of Thinking and Acting.* San Francisco: Jossey-Bass, 1987a.

Brookfield, S. D. "Cultural Literacy: A Cocktail Party View of Higher Education." *Chronicle of Higher Education,* 1987b, *34* (3), 43.

Brookfield, S. D. "Analyzing the Influence of Media on Learners' Perspectives." In J. Mezirow and Associates, *Fos-*

*tering Critical Reflection in Adulthood: A Guide to Trans-formative and Emancipatory Learning.* San Francisco: Jossey-Bass, 1990a.

Brookfield, S. D. "Grounding Teaching in Learning." In M. Galbraith (ed.), *Facilitating Adult Learning: A Transactional Process.* Melbourne, Fla.: Krieger, 1990b.

Brookfield, S. D. "Using Critical Incidents to Explore Learners' Assumptions." In J. Mezirow and Associates, *Fostering Critical Reflection in Adulthood: A Guide to Transformative and Emancipatory Learning.* San Francisco: Jossey-Bass, 1990c.

Brookfield, S. D. "Discussion." In M. Galbraith (ed.), *Adult Learning Methods.* Melbourne, Fla.: Krieger, 1990d.

Brown, G. A. *Lecturing and Explaining.* London: Methuen, 1980.

Brown, G. A. "Lectures and Lecturing." In M. J. Dunkin (ed.), *International Encyclopedia of Teaching and Teacher Education.* New York: Pergamon, 1987.

Brown, G. A., and Atkins, M. *Effective Teaching in Higher Education.* New York: Methuen, 1987.

Brown, G. A., and Bakhtar, M. A. (eds.). *Styles of Lecturing.* Loughborough: Loughborough University Press, 1983.

Brunner, E. de S., and others. *An Overview of Adult Education Research.* Chicago: Adult Education Association of the U.S.A., 1959.

Butterwick, S. "Re-entry for Women: This Time It's Personal." *Proceedings of the Adult Education Research Conference,* no. 29. Calgary: Faculty of Continuing Education, University of Calgary, 1988.

Calderhead, J. *Teachers' Classroom Decision Making.* New York: Holt, Rinehart & Winston, 1984.

Calderhead, J. (ed.). *Exploring Teachers' Thinking.* London: Cassell Educational, 1987.

Calderhead, J. (ed.). *Teachers' Professional Learning.* Philadelphia: Taylor & Francis, 1988.

Cervero, R. M. "A Framework for Effective Practice in Adult Education." *Proceedings of the Adult Education Research Conference,* no. 30. Madison: Department of Adult Education, University of Wisconsin–Madison, 1989.

Charnley, A. H., and Jones, H. A. *The Concept of Success in Adult Literacy.* London: Adult Literacy and Basic and Skills Unit, 1979.

Chené, A. "From the Text to the Adult Learning Trajectory." *Proceedings of the Adult Education Research Conference,* no. 29. Calgary: Faculty of Continuing Education, University of Calgary, 1988.

Clark, C. "Asking the Right Questions About Teacher Preparation: Contributions of Research on Teacher Thinking." *Educational Researcher,* 1988, *17* (2), 5–12.

Claxton, C. S., and Murrell, P. H. *Learning Styles: Implications for Improving Educational Practices.* ASHE-ERIC Higher Education Report, no. 4. Washington, D.C.: Association for the Study of Higher Education.

Cochran-Smith, M., and Lytle, S. L. "Research on Teaching and Teacher Research: The Issues That Divide." *Educational Researcher,* 1990, *19,* (2), 2–11.

Coggins, C. C. "Impact of Adults' Preferred Learning Styles and Perception of Barriers on Completion of External Baccalaureate Degree Programme." In M. Zukas (ed.), *Papers from the Transatlantic Dialogue.* Leeds: School of Continuing Education, University of Leeds, 1988.

Conti, C. J., and Fellenz, R. A. "Teacher Actions That Influence Native American Learners." In M. Zukas (ed.), *Papers from the Transatlantic Dialogue.* Leeds: School of Continuing Education, University of Leeds, 1988.

Daloz, L. A. *Effective Teaching and Mentoring: Realizing the Transformational Power of Adult Learning Experiences.* San Francisco: Jossey-Bass, 1986.

Daloz, L. A. "The Story of Gladys Who Refused to Grow." *Lifelong Learning,* 1988, *11* (4), 4–7.

D'Andrea, A. "Teachers and Reflection: A Description and Analysis of the Reflective Process Which Teachers Use in Their Experiential Learning." Unpublished doctoral dissertation, Department of Adult Education, Ontario Institute for Studies in Education, 1985.

Danis, C., and Tremblay, N. A. "Autodidactic Learning Experiences: Questioning Established Adult Learning Principles." In H. B. Long and Associates, *Self-Directed Learning: Application and Theory*. Athens, Ga.: Department of Adult Education, University of Georgia, 1988.

Denis, M. M. "Toward the Development of a Theory of Intuitive Learning in Adults Based on a Descriptive Analysis." Unpublished doctoral dissertation, Department of Adult Education, Ontario Institute for Studies in Education, 1979.

Eble, K. E. *The Aims of College Teaching*. San Francisco: Jossey-Bass, 1983.

Eble, K. E. *The Craft of Teaching: A Guide to Mastering the Professors's Art*. (2nd ed.) San Francisco: Jossey-Bass, 1988.

Edwards, J. *Working Class Adult Education in Liverpool: A Radical Approach*. Manchester: Center for Adult and Higher Education, University of Manchester, 1986.

Elbow, P. *Embracing Contraries: Explorations in Teaching and Learning*. New York: Oxford University Press, 1986.

Elsey, B. "Mature Students' Experiences of University." *Studies in Adult Education*, 1982, *14* (1), 69–77.

Entwistle, N., and Ramsden, P. *Understanding Student Learning*. New York: Nichols, 1983.

Ericksen, S. C. *The Essence of Good Teaching: Helping Students Learn and Remember What They Learn*. San Francisco: Jossey-Bass, 1984.

Essert, P. L. "The Discussion Group in Adult Education in America." In M. L. Ely (ed.), *Handbook of Adult Education in the United States*. New York: Teachers College Press, 1948.

Finger, M. "The Biographical Method in Adult Education Research." *Studies in Continuing Education*, 1989, *10* (2), 33–42.

Fink, L. D. *The First Year of College Teaching*. New Directions for Teaching and Learning, no. 17. San Francisco: Jossey-Bass, 1984.

Freire, P. *Pedagogy of the Oppressed*. New York: Continuum, 1970.

Gamson, Z. F., and Associates. *Liberating Education*. San Francisco: Jossey-Bass, 1984.

Gehrels, C. "The School Principal as Learner." Unpublished doctoral dissertation, Department of Adult Education, Ontario Institute for Studies Education, 1984.

Giroux, H. A. *Theory and Resistance in Education: A Pedagogy for the Opposition.* Granby, Mass.: Bergin & Garvey, 1983.

Giroux, H. A. *Teachers as Intellectuals: Toward a Critical Pedagogy of Learning.* Granby, Mass.: Bergin & Garvey, 1988.

Glaser, B. G., and Strauss, A. L. *The Discovery of Grounded Theory: Strategies for Qualitative Research.* Chicago: Aldine, 1967.

Goldschmid, M. "Parrainage: Students Helping Each Other." In D. Boud (ed.), *Developing Student Autonomy in Learning.* (2nd ed.) New York: Nichols, 1988.

Goodlad, J. I., Soder, R., and Sirotnik, K. A. *The Moral Dimensions of Teaching.* San Francisco: Jossey-Bass, 1990.

Goodlad, S., and Hirst, B. *Peer Tutoring: A Guide to Learning by Teaching.* New York: Nichols, 1989.

Graff, A. O., and Coggins, C. C. "Twenty Voices—Reflections on Pursuing an External Baccalaureate Degree." *Proceedings of the Adult Education Research Conference,* no. 30. Madison: Department of Continuing and Vocational Education, University of Wisconsin–Madison, 1989.

Greenblatt, C. S. *Designing Games and Simulations.* Newbury Park, Calif.: Sage, 1988.

Greene, M. "In Search of a Critical Pedagogy," *Harvard Educational Review,* 1986, *56* (4), 427–441.

Griffith, G. "Images of Interdependence: Meaning and Movement in Teaching/Learning." Unpublished doctoral dissertation, Department of Adult Education, Ontario Institute for Studies in Education, 1982.

Grossman, J. "Journal Writing and Adult Learning: A Naturalistic Study." Unpublished doctoral dissertation. Program in Human and Organizational Development, Fielding Institute, Santa Barbara, 1988.

Hayes, E. (ed.). *Effective Teaching Styles.* New Directions for Continuing Education, no. 43. San Francisco: Jossey-Bass, 1989.

Hirsch, E. D., Jr. *Cultural Literacy: What Every American Needs to Know.* Boston: Houghton Mifflin, 1987.

Hoadley, M. R., and Vik, P. A. "Effective College Teaching."

In R. L. Emans (ed.), *Understanding Undergraduate Education*. Lanham, Md.: University Press of America, 1989.

Holly, M. L. *Keeping a Personal-Professional Journal*. Victoria, Australia: Deakin University Press, 1987.

Hutchinson, E., and Hutchinson, E. *Women Returning to Learning*. Cambridge, England: National Extension College, 1988.

Jackson, P. *The Study of Teaching*. New York: Teachers College Press, 1986.

Jackson, P. *Life in Classrooms*. New York: Teachers College Press, 1990.

Jersild, A. *When Teachers Face Themselves*. New York: Teachers College Press, 1955.

Jones, K. *Designing Your Own Simulations*. New York: Methuen, 1985.

Jones, K. *Interactive Learning Events: A Guide for Facilitators*. New York: Nichols, 1988.

Katz, J. (ed.). *Teaching as Though Students Mattered*. New Directions for Teaching and Learning, no. 21. San Francisco: Jossey-Bass, 1985.

Keane, R. "The Experience of Doubt and Associated Learning in Religious Men." Unpublished doctoral dissertation, Department of Adult Education, Ontario Institute for Studies in Education, 1985.

Kennedy, W. B. "Integrating Personal and Social Ideologies." In J. Mezirow and Associates, *Fostering Critical Reflection in Adulthood: A Guide to Emancipatory and Transformative Learning*. San Francisco: Jossey-Bass, 1990.

Kolb, D. A. "Learning Styles and Disciplinary Differences." In A. W. Chickering and Associates, *The Modern American College: Responding to the New Realities of Diverse Students and a Changing Society*. San Francisco: Jossey-Bass, 1981.

Kolb, D. A. "Future Directions for Learning Style Research." In L. Curry (ed.), *Learning Style in Continuing Medical Education*. Ottowa: Canadian Medical Association, 1983.

Kolb, D. A. *Experiential Learning: Experience as the Source of Learning and Development*. Englewood Cliffs, N.J.: Prentice-Hall, 1984.

Lewis, L. H. (ed.). *Experiential and Simulation Techniques for Teaching Adults.* New Directions for Continuing Education, no. 30. San Francisco: Jossey-Bass, 1986.

Lindeman, E.C.L. "World Peace Through Adult Education." *Nation's Schools,* 1945, *35* (3), 23.

Lodge, D. *Nice Work.* Harmondsorth, England: Penguin, 1989.

Lowman, J. *Mastering the Techniques of Teaching.* San Francisco: Jossey-Bass, 1984.

Lukinsky, J. "Reflective Withdrawal Through Journal Writing." In J. Mezirow and Associates, *Fostering Critical Reflection in Adulthood: A Guide to Transformative and Emancipatory Learning.* San Francisco: Jossey-Bass, 1990.

McKeachie, W. J. *Teaching Tips: A Guide for the Beginning College Teacher.* (8th ed.) Lexington, Mass.: Heath, 1986.

Maclaren, A. *Ambitions and Realizations: Women in Adult Education.* Washington, D.C.: Peter Owen, 1986.

Marton, F., Hounsell, D., and Entwistle, N. (eds.). *The Experience of Learning.* Edinburgh: Scottish Academic Press, 1984.

Meyers, C. *Teaching Students to Think Critically: A Guide for Faculty in All Disciplines.* San Francisco: Jossey-Bass, 1986.

Mezirow, J. "Perspective Transformation." *Studies in Adult Education,* 1977, *9* (2), 153–164.

Mezirow, J., and Associates. *Fostering Critical Reflection in Adulthood: A Guide to Transformative and Emancipatory Learning.* San Francisco: Jossey-Bass, 1990.

Millar, C., Morphett, T., and Saddington, T. "Curriculum Negotiation in Professional Adult Education." *Journal of Curriculum Studies,* 1986, *18* (4), 429–443.

Milroy, E. *Role Play: A Practical Guide.* Aberdeen: Aberdeen University Press, 1982.

Modra, H. "Using Learning Journals to Encourage Critical Thinking at a Distance." In T. Evans and D. Nation (eds.), *Critical Reflection in Distance Education.* Philadelphia: Taylor & Francis, 1989.

Moustakas, C. *The Authentic Teacher: Sensitivity and Awareness in the Classroom.* Cambridge, Mass.: Howard A. Doyle, 1966.

Paterson, R.W.K. "The Concept of Discussion: A Philosophical Approach." *Studies in Adult Education,* 1970, *1* (2), 28–50.

Perry, W. G. "Different Worlds in the Same Classroom." In P. Ramsden (ed.), *Improving Learning: New Perspectives.* New York: Nichols, 1988.

Persico, C. "Non-Traditional Technical Programs for Women: Barriers and Facilitators to Learning." Unpublished doctoral dissertation, Department of Higher and Adult Education, Teachers College, Columbia University, 1988.

Pratt, D. D. "Cross-Cultural Relevance of Selected Psychological Perspectives on Learning." In M. Zukas (ed.), *Papers from the Transatlantic Dialogue.* Leeds: School of Continuing Education, University of Leeds, 1988a.

Pratt, D. D. "Three Perspectives on Teacher Effectiveness." *Proceedings of the Adult Education Research Conference,* no. 29. Calgary: Faculty of Continuing Education, University of Calgary, 1988b.

Pratt, D. D. "Culture and Learning: A Comparison of Western and Chinese Conceptions of Self and Individuality." *Proceedings of the Adult Education Research Conference,* no. 30. Madison: Department of Continuing and Vocational Education, University of Wisconsin–Madison, 1989.

Rannells Saul, J. "Women Speak About Their Learning Experiences in Higher Education." *Proceedings of the Adult Education Research Conference,* no. 30. Madison: Department of Continuing and Vocational Education, University of Wisconsin–Madison, 1989.

Robinson, J., Saberton, S., and Griffin, V. (eds.). *Learning Partnerships: Interdependent Learning in Adult Education.* Toronto: Department of Adult Education, Ontario Institute for Studies in Education, 1985.

Rogers, C. R. *A Way of Being.* Boston: Houghton Mifflin, 1980.

Rogers, J. *Adults Learning.* (3rd ed.) Philadelphia: Open University Press, 1989.

Ross, J. M., and Pena, M. "Critical Teaching Behaviors as Perceived by Returning Adult College Students." *Proceedings of the Adult Education Research Conference,* no. 29. Calgary: Faculty of Continuing Education, University of Calgary, 1988.

Salzberger-Wittenberg, I., Henry, G., and Osborne, E. *The Emotional Experience of Teaching and Learning.* New York: Routledge, Chapman & Hall, 1983.

Schön, D. A. *The Reflective Practitioner: How Professionals Think in Action.* New York: Basic Books, 1983.

Shaw, M. E., Corsini, R., Blake, R. R., and Mouton, J. S. *Role Playing: A Practical Manual for Group Facilitators.* San Diego, Calif.: University Associates, 1982.

Sheckley, B. G. "The Best and Worst Classroom Learning Experiences of Adult Learners." In M. Zukas (ed.), *Papers from the Transatlantic Dialogue.* Leeds: School of Continuing Education, University of Leeds, 1988.

Shor, I. *Culture Wars: School and Society in the Conservative Restoration, 1969–1984.* New York: Routledge, Chapman & Hall, 1986.

Shor, I. *Critical Teaching and Everyday Life.* Chicago: University of Chicago Press, 1987.

Shor, I., and Freire, P. A. *Pedagogy for Liberation: Dialogues on Transforming Education.* Granby, Mass.: Bergin & Garvey, 1987.

Smyth, W. J. *A Rationale for Teachers' Critical Pedagogy: A Handbook.* Victoria, Australia: Deakin University Press, 1986.

Snow, C. P. *The Masters.* New York: Macmillan, 1951.

Snow, C. P. *The Corridors of Power.* New York: Macmillan, 1964.

Spear, G. "Beyond the Organizing Circumstance: A Search for Methodology for the Study of Self-Directed Learning." In H. B. Long and Associates, *Self-Directed Learning: Application and Theory.* Athens: Department of Adult Education, University of Georgia, 1988.

Spear, G., and Mocker, D. "The Organizing Circumstance: Environmental Determinants in Self-Directed Learning." *Adult Education Quarterly,* 1984, *35* (1), 1–10.

Tarule, J. M. "Voices of Returning Women: Ways of Knowing." In L. H. Lewis (ed.), *Addressing the Needs of Return-*

*ing Women.* New Directions for Continuing Education, no. 39. San Francisco: Jossey-Bass, 1988.

Taylor, M. "Adult Learning in an Emergent Learning Group: Toward a Theory of Learning from the Learner's Perspective." Unpublished doctoral dissertation, Department of Adult Education, Ontario Institute for Studies in Education, 1979.

Tom, A. *Teaching as a Moral Craft.* New York: Longman, 1984.

Topping, K. *The Peer Tutoring Handbook: Promoting Co-operative Learning.* Cambridge, Mass.: Brookline Books, 1988.

Tripp, D. H. *Theorizing Practice: The Teacher's Professional Journal.* Victoria, Australia: Deakin University Press, 1987.

Tulasiewicz, W., and Adams, A. (eds.). *Teacher's Expectations and Teaching Reality.* New York: Routledge, Chapman & Hall, 1989.

Van Ments, M. *The Effective Use of Role Play: A Handbook for Teachers and Trainers.* (2nd ed.) New York: Nichols, 1989.

Van Tilburg, E., and DuBois, J. E. "Literacy Students' Perceptions of Successful Participation in Adult Education: A Cross-Cultural Approach Through Expectancy-Valence." *Proceedings of the Adult Education Research Conference,* no. 30. Madison: Department of Continuing and Vocational Education, University of Wisconsin–Madison, 1989.

Watkins, R. "Co-operative Learning in Discussion Groups." *Teaching at a Distance,* 1975, *2* (1), 7–9.

Weimer, M. *Improving College Teaching: Strategies for Instructional Effectiveness.* San Francisco: Jossey-Bass, 1990.

Whitman, N. A. *Peer Teaching: To Teach Is to Learn Twice.* ASHE-ERIC Higher Education Report, no. 4. Washington, D.C.: Association for the Study of Higher Education, 1988.

Woodley, A., and others. *Choosing to Learn: Adults in Education.* Philadelphia: Open University Press, 1987.

Woods, P., and Sykes, P. J. "The Use of Teacher Biographies in Professional Self-Development." In F. Todd (ed.), *Planning Continuing Professional Development.* New York: Routledge, Chapman & Hall, 1987.

# Index